OECD
SOCIETIES
IN TRANSITION

The future of work and leisure

ORGANISATION FOR ECONOMIC CO-OPERATION AND DEVELOPMENT

ORGANISATION FOR ECONOMIC CO-OPERATION AND DEVELOPMENT

Pursuant to Article 1 of the Convention signed in Paris on 14th December 1960, and which came into force on 30th September 1961, the Organisation for Economic Co-operation and Development (OECD) shall promote policies designed:

— to achieve the highest sustainable economic growth and employment and a rising standard of living in Member countries, while maintaining financial stability, and thus to contribute to the development of the world economy;
— to contribute to sound economic expansion in Member as well as non-member countries in the process of economic development; and
— to contribute to the expansion of world trade on a multilateral, non-discriminatory basis in accordance with international obligations.

The original Member countries of the OECD are Austria, Belgium, Canada, Denmark, France, Germany, Greece, Iceland, Ireland, Italy, Luxembourg, the Netherlands, Norway, Portugal, Spain, Sweden, Switzerland, Turkey, the United Kingdom and the United States. The following countries became Members subsequently through accession at the dates indicated hereafter: Japan (28th April 1964), Finland (28th January 1969), Australia (7th June 1971), New Zealand (29th May 1973) and Mexico (18th May 1994). The Commission of the European Communities takes part in the work of the OECD (Article 13 of the OECD Convention).

Publié en français sous le titre :
LES SOCIÉTÉS DE L'OCDE EN TRANSITION :
L'AVENIR DU TRAVAIL ET DES LOISIRS

Foreword

The long-term outlook for employment in the OECD area is not encouraging. Most of the government agencies and research institutes involved in long-range labour market projections expect high levels of unemployment – which currently stands at around 35 million, or 8½ per cent of the OECD workforce – to persist well into the next decade. In addition, many millions of people will be underemployed or, discouraged by the lack of job opportunities, will have dropped out of the labour market. Over the coming period, most jobs will undergo important transformations, as indeed will the way work is organised. Clearly, such enormous changes will have a major impact not only on leisure and education, but also on family and community life. Are OECD societies sufficiently adaptable to deal with such pressures without sacrificing social cohesion?

To examine these issues, and also to add a longer-term societal dimension to the work on *The OECD Jobs Study* under way at the time, the OECD organised early in 1994 a "Forum for the Future" conference. The overall objective of the meeting was to evaluate likely long-term developments in employment and unemployment, and to explore the opportunities and risks that changes in work and in society may bring OECD countries in the decades ahead.

The meeting consisted of four sessions. The first assessed the longer-term outlook for growth and employment over the next ten to fifteen years or so, especially in the OECD area. It paid particular attention to the driving forces and assumptions underlying recent projections by various research institutes. The second session was devoted to an assessment of where the number of jobs is likely to expand or decline, to the changes in occupations and job profiles that can be expected in the coming years, and to the ensuing challenges for education and training, and for government policy more generally. The third focused on the changing relationship of work, leisure and other non-work-related activities, and how these are affected by shifting societal values. The final session examined the issue of social cohesion in OECD countries, the pressures bearing on traditional social structures, and new developments in social organisation which could contribute positively to the future evolution of OECD societies.

This publication brings together the papers presented at the meeting, as well as an introductory contribution by the Secretariat. The book is made available on the responsibility of the Secretary-General of the OECD.

Table of Contents

Long-term Prospects for Work and Social Cohesion in OECD Countries:
An Overview of the Issues
by *Barrie Stevens and Wolfgang Michalski*   7

The Long-term Outlook for Growth and Employment
by *Emilio Fontela*   25

Workforce 2005: The Future of Jobs in the United States and Europe
by *Alan Reynolds*   47

Value Changes and the Achieving Society: A Social-philosophical Perspective
by *Hans Lenk*   81

Prospects of Social Cohesion in OECD Countries
by *Christian Lutz*   95

Annex: List of Participants 121

Long-term Prospects for Work and Social Cohesion in OECD Countries: An Overview of the Issues

by

Barrie Stevens and Wolfgang Michalski
OECD Secretariat, Advisory Unit to the Secretary-General

Social cohesion in OECD countries is under increasing pressure, not least from the current high levels of unemployment. Without counting the many workers who are underemployed, in early retirement, or not captured by the statistics, in 1994 an average of some 35 million people will be without jobs in the OECD area. Indeed, since the early 1970s, there has been an upward drift in unemployment in most Member countries. The largest trend increase in joblessness, and also the most acute problems of long-term unemployment, have been seen in the European Community, Australia and New Zealand; the average unemployment rate has also been relatively high in North America, although the trend increase over the period has been modest; in the EFTA countries, unemployment has picked up sharply since 1990. Only in Japan has it remained generally low, but even there it now seems to be on the rise.

Looking further ahead, the international and domestic economic forces that have been putting so much pressure on OECD labour markets – and indeed on societies more generally – seem very likely to continue. Not surprisingly, therefore, long-term projections by a variety of research institutions and international organisations suggest that high unemployment could be here for the foreseeable future. Then again, long-term projections are inherently uncertain. Their main purpose is to highlight the risks and opportunities facing the economy and society over the coming years, as well as the need to examine different policy options. Projected trends are not to be regarded as an inevitability. After all, the future is there to be shaped.

1. The outlook for growth and employment

Projections of various institutes (*e.g.* the US Bureau of Labor Statistics, the CEPII and OFCE in France, the Institut für Arbeitsmarkt- und Berufsforschung in Germany, the Netherlands Central Planning Bureau, Prognos in Switzerland, the Japan Center for

Economic Research) suggest on aggregate that the labour force in the OECD area is set to grow over the next ten to fifteen years at an average annual rate of less than 1 per cent. This is much slower than the growth rates of the last two decades. In terms of absolute numbers, there will be wide variations in workforce growth among the countries and major regions of the OECD. While in the United States the net increase between 1992 and 2005 is expected to be of the order of 24 million people (a total increase over the period of 19 per cent), Japan will only add some 4 million (a total net increase of only 6 per cent). Over the same period, EC Europe could see its labour force expand by some 10 million workers (a rise of 6 to 7 per cent).

These projections are highly sensitive to changes in underlying assumptions, particularly those pertaining to the size of the working-age population – itself often determined to an important degree by migration – and to labour market participation rates. Thus, in the Bureau of Labor Statistics growth projection for the US workforce by the middle of the next decade, alternative scenarios based on different hypotheses generate outcomes that differ by a margin of 9 million people, *i.e.* over 7 per cent of the current workforce. The Bureau estimates that over two-thirds of this divergence is attributable to differing assumptions about the inflow of migrant workers; clearly, for countries with high and fluctuating immigration (legal and illegal), forecasting workforce size is a delicate exercise.

Labour market participation rates have in the past few decades become a complex matter. Generally speaking, rates have increased very substantially for women while they have fallen for men, especially for the older age groups. However, it should be kept in mind that the very notion of participation has become increasingly imprecise with the spread of part-time and non-regular forms of employment. Still, this complexity in no way diminishes the importance of rate changes for workforce projections. Over the 1980s, one-sixth of OECD labour force growth was due to rising participation. And in a recent analysis of the long-term outlook for the EC labour market, Eurostat develops two ''not unrealistic'' scenarios to the end of the next decade, the results of which diverge by almost 10 million workers. The calculations demonstrate that at least as far as EC Europe is concerned, the effects of changing participation rates on the size of the labour force could in fact swamp any effects emanating from demographic growth.

Changes in participation rates in turn depend on a wide range of factors, *e.g.* government policies on retirement, shifting social values with respect to remunerated work, the rise of part-time and temporary employment, changing patterns of secondary and tertiary education, and military service. To a very important extent, however, they also depend on the level of economic activity, with a booming economy inciting hitherto non-active persons to look for work, and a recession discouraging many people from job-seeking.

There is fairly broad agreement among the various institutions on the longer-term prospects for economic growth in the major OECD regions. The outlook is one of rather modest performance. Projections for the 1990s and first half of the next decade are in the 2 to 2½ per cent per annum range for the United States and Europe, while for Japan they cluster around 3 per cent, giving an aggregate estimate for the OECD area as a whole of around 2½ per cent. These admittedly very approximate figures are somewhat lower than those projected two to three years ago – no doubt a reflection of the generally poor economic performance of OECD countries since the early 90s and the somewhat sombre short-term prospects at the time the new projections were written.

Against this projected backcloth of generally mediocre economic performance to 2005-2010, and taking account of the rather poor employment record in recent years in numerous OECD countries (especially in Europe), many institutes (*e.g.* the National Institute for Economic and Social Research and the Institute for Employment Research in the United Kingdom, the French CEPII and OFCE, Prognos of Switzerland) paint a bleak picture as regards the job market in the years to come. They generally expect unemployment in EC Europe to remain at around 11 per cent until the end of the decade, with even higher rates persisting in France and Italy (12-14 per cent) and in Spain and Ireland (15-18 per cent). In some Nordic countries as well, unemployment is likely to remain quite high over the period (Finland 12-13 per cent, Sweden 7-8 per cent). US rates of joblessness are projected to fluctuate around the 6-7 per cent mark, and those for Canada around 10 per cent; it is thought that Japan's rate could top 3 per cent.

In addition to the unemployed, there will be considerable numbers of people who are underemployed, *i.e.* involuntarily working part-time or on stop-gap training courses, or departed from the labour market because they consider further job-search futile and/or they have been encouraged by generous income support such as early retirement and disability schemes. The numbers of discouraged workers and those on involuntary part-time are already substantial (an estimated 13 million in the OECD area) and could well prove a persistent feature of the coming years. For Germany, for example, it is estimated that by the year 2000 there could be a "hidden reserve" of 2.6 million such underemployed on top of the projected 3.3 million registered unemployed. And there are reports that Japanese companies are carrying surplus labour of the order of $2\frac{1}{2}$ million (equivalent to about 3.8 per cent of the workforce).

Although a significant portion of current and projected unemployment is structural, there is little doubt that some of it is cyclical. Part of the solution may therefore lie in sustained recovery. Simulations by CEPII/OFCE show, for instance, that for EC Europe a growth rate of 5 per cent per annum could pull average unemployment back to 5 per cent by the end of the year 2000. However, for many countries, the annual real growth rates required for that aggregate average seem, from today's perspective at least, quite out of reach (*e.g.* almost 6 per cent for France, over 7 per cent for Spain, well over 8 per cent for Ireland). Many OECD countries face macroeconomic constraints which, due to strong trade and financial interdependencies, are mutually reinforcing. At the same time, governments do not have very much fiscal room for stimulating growth. Social expenditures and – with the notable exception of Japan – already high public debt burdens are set to rise in the major OECD economies to levels of around 50 per cent of GDP by the beginning of the next century.

Ongoing structural change will ensure that some countries and some sectors will expand or decline faster than others. There is a fair measure of agreement among long-term projections for Member countries on the favourable prospects for services, in particular those related to management, computers and data processing, accountancy, legal affairs, health and social matters, and entertainment and leisure activities, including tourism. The shares of the primary sector and of manufacturing in GDP will probably continue to fall, driven largely by declines in such sectors as agriculture, mining, foot-wear, textiles and clothing, leather goods, metals, household appliances and, with perhaps the exception of Japan, motor vehicles and office machines. Within the manufacturing sector, however, significant expansion is forecast for a number of activities, *e.g.* electronics, chemicals, medical equipment, pharmaceutics and cosmetics, and certain specialised sectors such as environmental protection equipment.

In exploring the future implications of these trends for employment, the distinction between manufacturing and services is quite artificial. A large number of jobs in manufacturing are in fact nonmanufacturing, service-type activities – engineering, design, sales and marketing, distribution, etc. Their share of manufacturing employment is thought to be as high as 70-80 per cent in countries such as the United States and Germany. The uncertainties surrounding future changes in manufacturing employment are, therefore, considerable. Sustained competitive pressure (both technology- and wage-driven) from developing countries and among OECD countries themselves could produce significant locational shifts of manufacturing activities over the coming years, affecting both traditional production jobs and related service-type jobs.

While non-traded services are clearly set to expand, the traded services sector in OECD countries is likely to face a much tougher environment. For example, a perfectly plausible scenario could be constructed in which the combined effect of a unified market and associated rapid productivity gains leads to a massive employment shake-out in European banking, insurance, financial services and transport. Similarly, offshore information processing could expand dramatically as the infrastructure for electronic data transmission between industrialised and developing countries is extended. Some experts believe that in a few years' time, up to 70 per cent of all such data processing could be relocated in countries such as Singapore, Taiwan, the Philippines and India.

With respect to prospects for the global economic environment as a whole, however, there are also grounds for optimism. Strong growth poles are emerging in Asia and Latin America, and these should provide vast markets as they expand. Also, a vital long-term boost has been given to the world economy with the successful conclusion of the Uruguay Round and NAFTA, and with the consolidation of the European Single Market. Moreover, it is important not to underestimate the internal dynamics of OECD economies: advances in product and process technology, the spread of more flexible systems of production and service provision, more innovative patterns of work organisation and locational strategy could help Member countries maintain and extend their international competitive position. In particular, the trend towards specialised custom-tailored production may enable them to regain comparative advantages lost to developing countries in recent decades; small and medium-size enterprises have great potential in this regard. Finally, demographic trends are likely to exert a largely positive influence on economic development in the next decades, in the form of new markets for products and services required by an ageing but wealthy population.

2. The profile of future jobs

Recent long-term projections for OECD countries tend to agree on the broad categories of occupations for which demand over the next ten years or so is likely to be strong (professional, technical, administrative and managerial occupations) or weak (agricultural, production and labouring occupations). However, there are important variations within these broad categories.

In the United States, which is expected to generate 24 million new net jobs between 1992 and 2005, the biggest increases will probably occur in certain personal services-related occupations. No doubt because of the country's changing demographic composition, five of the ten fastest-growing occupations involve the delivery of medical services: home health aides, personal and home care aides, physical therapists, physical and corrective therapy assistants, and medical assistants. In terms of absolute numbers, registered nurses and nursing aides, orderlies, etc. could account for a net growth of over 1.3 million jobs. However, considerable growth is also expected in jobs related to the expansion in information and computer technologies, notably systems analysts and computer scientists. Broadly similar trends are projected for other OECD countries such as Australia, Germany, the Netherlands and Japan.

The sharpest declines look set to occur among farmers and agricultural workers, textile, clothing and leather workers, electrical equipment assemblers, and clerks involved in routine office operations. Again, this represents a fairly general trend across many countries.

Changing job profiles raise important questions about the qualifications of the workforce needed to fill job opportunities, and indeed about many other characteristics of the future labour force. The vast majority of projections of this type point to developments which have long become conventional wisdom: notwithstanding a certain arbitrariness of occupational classifications, a great number of jobs in which rapid expansion is expected will be in highly qualified, well-paid occupations, and the most significant declines will probably be in some of the traditional low-skill, low-paid occupations. This is not to say, however, that there will likely be a generalised shortage of jobs for the low-skilled. On the contrary, in the non-traded goods sector and particularly in personal services, considerable job growth may occur. In the United States, for example, salespersons, cashiers, food preparation workers, waiters and waitresses could together account for a net addition to the workforce of 2.6 million jobs by 2005, and over the same period occupations such as guards, gardeners and groundsmen are expected to add a further 700 000.

Linking these overall trends with the evolving demographic, social and ethnic composition of the OECD workforce highlights a number of problematic issues.

First, there is the changing demographic composition of OECD societies. In almost all countries, the next ten to fifteen years will see fewer young people entering the labour force. In the United States, the proportion of 25- to 34-year-olds will decline by about 5 per cent by 2005; the share of 15- to 29-year-old Japanese in the workforce is set to fall from 23 per cent in 1990 to 17.5 per cent in 2010; and in EC Europe, the average share of under-35s will decline from 40.4 per cent to 36 per cent by the end of the decade, with much steeper decreases of around 7 percentage points for the Netherlands, Germany and Belgium. At the same time, OECD workforces will be ageing, with the share of older workers growing considerably into the next decade. This is good news in the sense that they embody experience and skills, earn higher incomes, save more, pay more taxes, etc.

However, faced with a rapidly transforming spectrum of job profiles and qualification requirements, Member countries will find themselves with fewer young people to replenish the skills pool, and an older workforce that could have a reduced capacity for mobility, flexibility and learning – and possibly greater resistance to change.

Secondly, in some countries there is evidence of a polarisation between low-qualification, low-paid jobs on the one hand and high-qualification, high-income jobs on the other, which is compounded by (or perhaps reflected in) widening earnings differentials and, at least in the United States, a shrinking middle-income bracket in the population. For many observers this is related to a ''hollowing out'' of traditional, middle-income blue collar and white collar jobs. In the past, such work has offered a career path and a reasonably predictable and stable income which formed the basis for durable consumption and investment decisions characteristic of middle-class life. Even more importantly perhaps, such jobs traditionally provided the main pathways for inter-generational mobility. The concern is that such channels of upward social mobility are gradually being closed off, a phenomenon with consequences for both the stability and the dynamic evolution of society.

Finally, there are signs of increasing diversity in the labour force of OECD countries in terms of the size of ethnic groups, presence of foreign nationals, etc. In the United States, for example, the share of Blacks and Hispanics in the labour force will continue to rise, from the current level of about 18 per cent to 22 per cent in 2005. While it is true that both the average level and the average years of schooling among these groups has risen, they still tend to have the lowest educational attainment and to be disproportionately employed in sectors and occupations already in sharp decline; they are therefore more vulnerable to changing employment and qualification requirements than other population groups. In addition, there is evidence – albeit controversial – that the skill level of immigrants entering the United States and Canada between the 1960s and 1980s deteriorated relative to that of native North Americans, largely due to the changing mix of immigration (an increasing share from poor developing countries). There are some encouraging signs in more recent statistics: for example, about 24 per cent of post-1980 immigrants to the United States have a bachelor's degree or higher, compared with 19 per cent of pre-1980 immigrants. However, it is thought that the impact of such improvements may be outweighed by the increasing number of immigrants (legal and illegal) with few or no qualifications who, given the declining number of Americans with less than a high school education, constitute a large share of the ''drop-out'' workforce.

One of the messages to emerge from this juxtaposition of projections and problems is that a major effort is called for on the education and training front in virtually all OECD countries. Changes in the composition of the workforce over the coming years – along with the growing internationalisation of the economy, further advances in technology, and the spread of new, innovative models of work organisation based on networking and greater personal autonomy – will demand substantial investment in human capital if the skill and qualification requirements of future jobs are to be met. The institutions, structures and practices of education and training thus face a number of specific long-term challenges in the next decades.

To begin with, it is increasingly apparent that the sheer diversity and complexity of the demands on the education and training systems of OECD countries are growing, and will continue to grow. Large sections of the population in many countries, not least certain poorly educated ethnic groups, will need to be targeted for the teaching of basic reading, writing and numerical skills. At the same time, demand will continue for intermediate qualifications and for highly specialised advanced training. Added to this are the increasing needs for the further education and training of older workers, indeed for lifelong learning: in the future, many people will find it necessary to change jobs and possibly professions several times in the course of their working lives. At the other end of the age scale is the need to improve the transition from school to work, and to equip young people with broad-based skills that will facilitate their mobility and flexibility in later life, provide them with the basis to adjust to new types of work organisation, and prepare them in general for the advent of ''the learning society''. This in turn is likely to expand demand for education outside the traditional teaching situations: self-instruction using a variety of knowledge sources and media, TV schools and colleges, consulting and counselling, learning in project teams, etc. Given such prospects, education authorities may see their role focus increasingly on ensuring that such diverse educational activities emerge within a framework that is effective, competitive, and above all transparent.

Furthermore, there needs to be a better balance between academic and vocational qualifications. Although substantial numbers of young people in the OECD area suffer from inadequate access to basic and secondary education, the overall trend over the last ten to fifteen years has been towards the prolongation of studies into post-secondary education and training. The expansion of capacity has been uneven, with growth in academically oriented studies at university level outpacing that in technical and voca-tional studies. Yet occupational projections for a number of countries suggest that the latter qualifications will be of great importance in the coming years. Figures for the United States, for instance, indicate rapid growth between 1992 and 2005 in professions requiring a college degree or higher (systems analysis, computer sciences, psychologists, management analysts, etc.). But they also point to strong growth in a host of occupations requiring vocational training: paralegals (86 per cent), medical assistants (71 per cent), radiologic technologists and technicians (63 per cent), and so on. In Germany, it is expected that the share of the workforce with apprenticeship, post-apprenticeship and advanced technical qualifications will increase by the year 2000 to around 70 per cent, up from 66 per cent in the late 1980s.

And finally, changing work patterns raise questions concerning access to training. Recent years have seen a surge in many countries in the growth of non-regular employ-ment – part-time or temporary work, fixed-term contracts, certain forms of self-employ-ment, etc. This trend seems set to continue. For example, part-time employment in the United Kingdom, which in 1990 already accounted for about 22 per cent of the labour force, is set to rise by a further 700 000 between 1991 and 2000. Similarly strong growth in non-regular employment is expected for a number of other countries. Yet evidence from the last decade or so indicates that: *i)* there is a link between the amount of enterprise-based skill training received by an employee and the length of his or her tenure; *ii)* too high a level of turnover does not facilitate the development of workplace skills; and *iii)* those workers who have a good level of initial education and training tend to benefit more from further education and training than those with no or low levels of qualifications. A major sustained effort is clearly required to improve and broaden access to training.

It is unlikely that progress will be achieved in any of these areas without strengthening the incentives facing the principal actors in the education and training market. Institutions will need encouragement to diversify their repertoire of courses so as to improve their responsiveness to the requirements of employers and employees alike. Workers' willingness to invest in their own training will need to be enhanced by ensuring that such training is as effective as possible in raising their incomes over the course of their working lives. Enterprises themselves are likely to demonstrate a greater preparedness to offer training if they are permitted to treat the accumulation of human capital within the firm as an investment on a par with physical capital, for example through provisions making investment in workforce training a tax-deductible expenditure.

3. New values associated with work and non-work-related activities

Leaving aside the more traditional labour market issues, it is useful to explore a number of broader societal developments which may enable all population groups to participate actively and constructively in the society of the 1990s and early 21st century. To begin with, OECD societies are set to become increasingly affluent in the years to come. Even assuming only moderate economic growth, per capita disposable personal incomes in the United States are likely to increase by one-quarter in real terms between 1990 and 2005, and in Japan real growth of disposable household incomes between 1990 and 2010 is projected to be in the order of 30 per cent. Increases of a similar magnitude are expected for many European countries. Added to this is the prospect for many families of inheriting the wealth accumulated by the postwar generation.

In the context of such a rise in prosperity, it is conceivable that wage-earners will become increasingly willing to contemplate working fewer hours. There has been a secular decline in average working hours in the industrialised countries: in Europe, for example, the average amount of time actually devoted to work has fallen from some 3 000 hours per year a century ago to around 1 700 today. Although over the past few decades the decline has tended to slow or level off, some OECD countries are projecting a renewed decline through the beginning of the next century. In Japan, for example, it is expected that average yearly working hours, after remaining fairly constant in the 1980s, will fall from their current level of 2 052 to 1 806 by the year 2010. Even countries with already relatively low average working hours foresee a similar trend. In Norway, for instance, working time per employee is projected to fall from about 1 400 hours in 1991 to around 1 300 in 2010.

Secondly, the findings of public opinion polls – national and international – indicate that important changes are taking place in people's views about work. They point to a fundamental shift in attitudes within advanced societies away from materialist values (such as economic and physical security) and towards what have been described as postmaterialist values, *i.e.* self-development, self-fulfilment, self-organisation, and aesthetic and intellectual orientations. This shift has gone hand in hand with a generally diminishing commitment to work among large – but by no means all – segments of the population. Even countries with a traditionally strong work ethic are not exempt from this overall trend. In both Germany and Japan, surveys have registered a perceptible decline in the level of personal commitment to work. In Japan, although work is still consistently ranked as highly important, it has for the first time in a long series of opinion polls been overtaken by the importance of the family in people's hierarchy of priorities. Clearly, however, the trend does not apply to all population groups.

The surveys find that on the whole, the declining attachment to work as a value is particularly pronounced among young people. However, it would be a mistake to infer from this the magnitude of value change which the younger generation is likely to introduce into society in future years. Indeed, young people are themselves often very conscious of the strong social and economic forces which will lead them to change their attitudes to work as they grow older. According to a recent survey, young Swedes attach a fairly high degree of importance to interesting work, but consider they would attach even more importance to it fifteen to twenty years hence. This in fact reflects a more general finding. An integral part of changing attitudes towards work is the growing importance attributed to its qualitative dimensions. For many people, greater autonomy at the workplace, the scope for co-operation and teamwork, and opportunities for further education and training weigh heavily in their assessment of work.

Rising prosperity, together with the widely observed shift in attitudes to work, opens up a range of opportunities in the search for solutions to some of the most pressing work- and society-related problems that OECD countries will face in the years to come. The combination creates more favourable conditions for a broad-based reconsideration of the potential of working time reductions and work-sharing. The two factors hold out the promise of broader acceptance within society of unremunerated activities, and offer the prospect of both work and leisure becoming accepted and respected sources of self- development and self-fulfilment.

The issue of work-sharing has not met with equal interest across the OECD area. What has emerged from the recent debate, however, is that a number of economic and political trends are making work-sharing a more viable prospect. First, as suggested above, substantial growth of real incomes in the years ahead for many of those in work will tend to augment the numbers of employees with sufficiently high earnings to allow them to countenance a trade-off between pay and working time. Secondly, there appears to be a more realistic acceptance on the part of some employees and some unions that sharing work implies sharing wages and should not lead to higher unit labour costs. There is, however, still strong resistance from many employers who fear that certain forms of working time reductions would, even with corresponding wage adjustments, undermine their competitive position. The general point to be made here is that legislated, across- the-board work-sharing is unlikely to be successful since it merely rations gainful work and imposes income cuts which will probably be resisted. Viable solutions are more likely to be found in voluntary, flexible arrangements which offer a diversity of options for reducing working time, *e.g.* various forms of leave (educational, parental, sabbatical) or the introduction of monthly or annual working hours.

Thirdly, and in line with the opinion polls described above, the popularity of work-sharing could be on the rise because people attach increasing value to time with the family or the pursuit of leisure activities. However, doubts persist not only about the practicability of work-sharing and its possible repercussions on overall economic growth, but also about its ability to deal with the root problems of unemployment. In the context of broader societal change, it may indeed be misguided to approach working time reduction and work-sharing primarily as an instrument for achieving a more just distribution of work, rather than as an avenue towards shaping society in a way that provides people with more free time to pursue non-work-related interests and to seek out new opportunities for self-development and self-fulfilment. The latter objective stands a greater chance of realisation if it is accompanied by moves toward more flexibility in other domains, *e.g.* through a loosening of some increasingly obsolete regulations governing work practices, shopping hours, etc. and a departure from the rigid division of the average week into working days and weekend.

A major obstacle to improving the social integration of the unemployed, underemployed, early retired, involuntary part-timers, etc. is that in today's societies work is not only a key source of income but also one of the most important means of achieving social recognition and status. Part of the problem is that despite rising affluence, OECD societies have so far been unable or unwilling to sever the link between gainful employment and acquisition of the basic physical and social necessities of life, for example through the introduction of universal minimum income schemes that would no longer carry the stigma of social transfers. Also important, however, is the role played by societal values. Broader public acknowledgement of activities outside the traditional concept of regular remunerated work – *e.g.* socially productive tasks for the community, volunteer work, improving the quality of the environment, and caring for children and the elderly – would considerably ease personal decisions to take up such opportunities.

The scope for the public authorities to bring about a reorientation of values in this respect is not as restricted as it may seem at first sight. Caring for the elderly is a case in point. In many OECD countries, the share of very elderly people being cared for in institutions has increased markedly, and the pressures on such institutions are set to rise. For example, over the period 1985-2025 the number of persons aged 80 and over is expected to increase in the developed world by some 22 million. At the same time, constraints on the financing of health care are very likely to tighten further. This suggests a need to focus more closely on home-based care services. A number of countries (*e.g.* Australia, Denmark, France, Japan, the Netherlands, the United Kingdom) have already taken initiatives on this front, introducing or improving allowances to people (usually members of the family) attending the elderly, placing less emphasis on services as an alternative to family care and more on seeking new forms of partnership between families and support services.

Not infrequently, of course, conflicting values get in the way of the best intentions. Japan is a case in point. Institutionalisation rates for the elderly have traditionally been low, with the family assuming most of the care-giving burden. But the prospect of rapid population ageing looms large on the not too distant horizon, threatening traditional patterns of care. Public opinion surveys indicate a widening gap between attitude and behaviour. More than 90 per cent of middle-aged Japanese believe that care of bedridden parents is the responsibility of the family – yet around half of the bedridden elderly are in fact in residential care. Part of the explanation for this contradiction seems to lie in the decline of the extended family, but also in the higher career aspirations and greater labour force participation of women.

For many people, in the years to come work will remain the principal vehicle of self-development and self-fulfilment, although the quality of their activities will likely undergo considerable change. In parallel with the technology-driven expansion of options for organising their work flexibly – telework, computerised offices, multimedia networking, etc. – they will typically attach considerable value to the immaterial attributes of work. These may include greater autonomy of action and decision at the workplace, the self-defining of roles and assignments, the desire to operate in an environment of co-operation, flexible working arrangements, and so on. For these people, the borderline between work and discretionary time will become increasingly blurred. In contrast, those workers who are unable to exploit such opportunities fully or at all may come to rely more on leisure and other non-work-related interests as a means of self-fulfilment. Such people are also typically likely to favour shorter and more flexible working arrangements, but primarily as a means to enlarge the scope for family life and leisure pursuits.

However, this projection of a ''leisure society'' is not without its problems. Continuation of present trends in a number of countries would ensure a very uneven distribution of capacity to exercise leisure activities, in two respects: *i)* some population groups have more discretionary time than others; and *ii)* the diversity of available leisure options, in particular the pursuit of cultural activities, correlates strongly with the level of education. Generally speaking, active people in the 20-50 age bracket constitute a group whose discretionary time is being squeezed between rising workloads on the one hand and studies on the other (women are often under additional strain due to family and household responsibilities). They stand in sharp contrast to those in the population who, because of unemployment, underemployment, disability or early retirement, find themselves with a lot of free time but not necessarily the means to translate that into self-development and self-fulfilment on the basis of leisure activities.

Of course, the benefits of expanded discretionary time to society as a whole depend to a considerable degree on the ''quality'' of leisure activities pursued as well as on broader access to leisure. Moreover, it is their qualitative content that largely determines the position of leisure pursuits on society's scale of values. As long as leisure's status remains much inferior to that accorded work, the full potential of leisure activities will remain unexploited. This poses a challenge to the education system, not only to help create an appropriate leisure culture but also to ensure through the teaching of creative and relational skills that people are able to take full advantage of the opportunities for self-fulfilment that such a culture might offer.

4. Cohesion in OECD societies

There is a fairly widespread perception that social cohesion in OECD societies is under threat from numerous sources. Many of these are external and relate mostly to the impacts of growing international economic and cultural interdependence. Some, however, are largely internal to OECD societies. First among these, perhaps, are the high and persistent levels of (especially long-term) unemployment and underemployment.

Second, poverty has been an enduring feature of recent decades in virtually all Member countries. It has proved in some countries to be remarkably resilient to improved overall economic performance. The United States has experienced constant and increasing poverty since about 1970; by conventional (normative) measures, some 35 million people are currently below the poverty threshold, a figure which represents about 14 per cent of the population. What is striking about the US situation is that almost 60 per cent of poor families have at least one member working – but against the background of falling relative wages, especially for low-skilled jobs, they do not earn enough to keep themselves above the poverty line. Moreover, it is estimated that for as many as one-third of all poor people, impoverishment is chronic (after three years, their income is still less than 50 per cent of the median income of the population as a whole). Particularly hard hit are Blacks and female-headed families. However, the picture of constant or rising poverty does not apply to the North American continent as a whole. Canada has been much more successful than its neighbour, bringing down its poverty rate (as measured by US definitions) by 45 per cent over the last twenty years, largely due to improvements in social transfers.

International comparative studies indicate that the incidence of poverty is generally lower in Europe than in North America, as also are cases of persistent poverty. It is thought that only a small fraction of the population in most European countries suffers severe hardship for more than three years running. Notable exceptions are to be found among ethnic minorities. The characteristics of the poor vary greatly across Europe. In some countries it is the retired or the very young householders who are chiefly at risk; in others it is single-parent families; in yet others the incidence of poverty is particularly marked among farmers. However, some characteristics feature consistently across the region. In general, households with no or only a weak attachment to the labour market (*e.g.* single-earner households) face a higher-than-average risk of poverty, a trend that has been aggravated by the sharp rise in recent years in the number of long-term unemployed. Moreover, for households other than the traditional family and/or where the head of household is divorced or separated, the risk is generally higher than average.

The modest prospects for economic growth, the poor state of government finances and the expected pruning of welfare spending mean it will be very difficult to make significant inroads into poverty over the next decade.

Third, to the extent that in some countries falling real wages, in particular for low-skilled workers, have contributed to locking people into poverty, widening earnings disparities are often perceived as a source of additional strain on the social fabric. A recent OECD study showed that in twelve of 17 OECD countries, earnings inequality increased in the 1980s. However, while the growth in disparities was quite substantial in the United States and United Kingdom, it was generally small in ten other countries, and in the remaining five the degree of inequality was roughly stable but often in relation to declines registered in the 1970s. Moreover, the rise in earnings inequality has not always gone hand in hand with growing family income disparities. Although this does appear to have been the case in the United States and the Netherlands (where post-transfer income inequalities actually increased faster than earnings inequalities) and to a lesser extent in the United Kingdom, other countries (*e.g.* Australia, Canada, France) have gone a long way towards offsetting the growth in earnings-related disparities through social transfers, albeit at considerable budgetary cost.

This touches on a fourth source of pressure on social cohesion, the issue of inter-generational redistribution. Fuelled by (*inter alia*) expanding coverage, demographic change and improvements in benefits, welfare budgets in OECD countries (for health, unemployment, pensions and other social benefits) have risen dramatically. The next few decades will see considerable increases in the numbers of elderly people. While the over-60s totalled around 100 million in 1990, their numbers are expected to increase to 115 million by the end of the decade, 130 million by 2010 and 156 million by 2020. The share of the working-age population available to support them will steadily decline, so that old-age dependency ratios will increase from 19 per cent in 1990 to 28 per cent in 2010 and 37 per cent ten years later. Some countries will feel the strain sooner than others. Japan and Germany, for example, will have age dependency ratios of 34 per cent already by 2010.

The severest impact of these demographic changes will be on pensions and health care budgets. Without increases in contributions, cuts in benefits and modifications to entitlements, the constraints on economic performance will become intolerable. But such reforms imply a significant redistribution of the financial burden and of benefits, both among the generations and among the different social groups, which could prove highly controversial. There are already concerns in some European countries that in the coming years health care priorities may shift towards alleviating the chronic ailments of the elderly, possibly at the expense of prevention programmes aimed at younger people. And in areas with large proportions of elderly, relatively wealthy people – Florida in the United States, for example – there is evidence of growing disaffection, particularly among the young, with the elderly residents' civic behaviour and impact on the community.

And fifth, OECD societies are becoming increasingly diverse; the last few years have seen a surge in immigration. In 1991 and 1992 alone, around 2 million immigrants are believed to have entered North America and Europe, and the projected increases in the population of the developing world are expected to contribute to the sustained immigration pressures from some countries well into the next century. For many OECD countries, immigration continues to be a vital source of economic prosperity and regener-ation, but there is concern in some quarters that Member countries' capacity to integrate growing migratory inflows may be weakening.

A significant obstacle in this respect appears to be the diminishing absorptive capacity of labour markets, especially in times of weak economic activity. Evidence from Canada, for example, suggests that while prior to 1965 complete assimilation (*i.e.* equal-ity of immigrants' earnings with those of native Canadians) within 15 years was the norm, since then absorption has taken longer and longer, with complete assimilation appearing to be out of reach for 1970s and 1980s immigrants. The steep decline in assimilation capability after 1981 is not thought to reflect increasing discrimination, since it applied to immigrants from the United States and Europe as well as those from Asia, Africa and Latin America. Furthermore, recent US studies of the impact of immigration from poorer countries show that it increases the supply of less-skilled workers, contributing significantly to rising earnings inequality overall. However, there is also the more general concern that migrants and certain resident ethnic groups face a potentially higher risk of poverty. Recent surveys indicate that in Germany, for example, both the incidence and the persistence of poverty are three times as likely to affect foreign residents as native Germans.

What emerges from this brief overview is that a number of divisive forces are at work which are combining to marginalise important albeit highly heterogeneous segments of the population in OECD societies. But weakening cohesion is also perceived as a wider problem than that of the materially disadvantaged, as evidenced by developments in other domains of public and private life. For example, recent years have witnessed a relative decline in the influence of established political parties and a proliferation of narrowly focused special interest groups, leading to fears that the capacity of the political system to develop and sustain coherent policy is being severely undermined. Moreover, with the widening sense of economic insecurity among many segments of the population, vested interests appear deeply entrenched. This in turn compounds the difficulty of implementing changes that would inject greater flexibility into much of the regulation and conventional thinking that tend to hamper broader adjustment within society to new developments.

The trend toward individualism has gained considerable momentum. At the same time, many young people seem to have experienced a loss of traditional value orientation. More extreme manifestations of this can be seen in the mounting body of evidence in the United States and United Kingdom that relates long-term youth unemployment with property crime. In parallel, the institutions which hitherto knitted together the social fabric have been undergoing important transformations. The role of families has changed, the influence of traditional structures of solidarity and consensus-building such as the Church and trade unions has declined, and the welfare state itself is being called into question. Thus traditional symbols of personal identification seem to be fading, leaving people with a strong sense of needing to "belong" and to participate, but with fewer means of expressing collective sovereignty, defining general interest, and structuring solidarity.

Perhaps the most dramatic change to have taken place these past forty years has been in the family. The extended family has become largely extinct, and the conventional two-parent, single-earner family is increasingly rare. Female participation rates have risen quite spectacularly, as have the numbers of single-parent families and single-person households. These trends are set to continue, even in the more traditional societies. In Japan, for example, female participation rates among 25- to 55-year-old women are expected to rise to well over 70 per cent by 2010, up from the current 55 per cent; the next fifteen to twenty years are also likely to see the share of single-person households increase from 21 to almost 28 per cent, that of extended families fall from 13 to 8 per cent, and divorce rates rise by some 60 per cent. Families in general will therefore be less capable of assuming certain social responsibilities, not least that of caring for the aged.

Opinion polls show the influence of the Church to be on the wane in many OECD countries, as attendance declines and the population's confidence in ecclesiastical institutions diminishes. Membership in trade unions has fallen significantly across the OECD area, affecting not only labour market developments such as wage negotiations and earnings differentials, but also those elements of collective agreements which relate to social arrangements, *e.g.* workers' compensation, health insurance, and pension provisions, many of which benefit workers who are not part of the union movement. At the same time, there is fairly widespread disenchantment with the established political parties and their ability to reflect changes in the ground swell of public opinion and its increasing diversity. And here lies a major problem for the marginalised groups of society: their very heterogeneity makes it extremely difficult for them to be heard by the established political parties and, conversely, makes it difficult for the political parties to address the underprivileged in a targeted, policy-relevant way.

Today, the most important institution of social protection and redistribution for many countries, the welfare state, is itself under siege. Support has been undermined by a variety of factors: *i)* the general increase in affluence, which has shifted the balance between those whose interests are best served by collectivism and those who most benefit from private solutions; *ii)* the increasing cost of social security benefits and the prospect of further substantial increases through demographic change; *iii)* the erosion of community forms of support; and *iv)* especially in periods of protracted weak growth, loss of economic support and confidence, which tend to undermine public support for collectivist welfare policies. Social and economic changes are making it increasingly unviable for the state to assume its responsibility for social welfare both financially and organisationally, while at the same time the traditional welfare bodies such as the Church and the family are increasingly incapable of filling the gap.

It is important, however, not to underestimate the internal dynamics of social systems. In some cases, self-correcting demographic mechanisms may be at work. Earnings disparities, for example, may begin to shrink again in some countries as the share of young people in the labour market declines in the next ten to fifteen years, their relative scarcity helping to push up their wages. The average level of education in the workforce will rise as older, less-educated workers retire, and the education level of most minorities will continue to rise. Moreover, many older people in the future will have accumulated considerable assets on retirement – partly through privately financed pension, insurance and other savings plans, partly through inherited wealth. In the United States, for instance, it is estimated that the baby boom generation will inherit around $10 trillion in current dollars.

On the unemployment front, there is clearly no single cure for the structural problems faced by OECD countries. Marked improvements can only be achieved through an accumulation of individual steps, many of them reaching beyond conventional measures related to the labour market and social policy. Their success, however, will depend heavily on political and economic factors. In particular, such measures would in all probability encounter obstacles in the form of diverse and deeply entrenched vested interests – although in some countries, especially in Europe, such obstacles may begin to recede as the Community becomes increasingly reluctant to countenance the social implications of chronically high and widespread unemployment, and increasingly favourable to the notion of a fundamental shift in policy away from income solidarity and towards more job solidarity.

Responses to financial hardship reveal that a growing diversity of "survival strategies" – complex work patterns, multiple part-time and even full-time job-holding, a blossoming of activities in the informal sector, and so on – coupled with take-up of available welfare benefits, allows many people on very low incomes to move out of their financially precarious situation. Thus, alongside of the observed persistence of hardship in many countries, there is evidence of relatively high rates of mobility out of poverty. International comparisons suggest that in a given year, the fraction of families in the bottom income decile who escape poverty by the following year is around 25 per cent in North America, France, Germany, Ireland and the Netherlands.

For many observers, growing individualism is a key factor underlying the erosion of conventional family structures and solidarity. Yet, freedom of choice and a wider radius of individual action are to be welcomed in so far as they broaden the range of work opportunities for men and women, extend the options for a more rewarding mix of activities related to work, leisure, family and the community, and enlarge the scope for autonomy and self-development.

Moreover, there are indications that the concept of family, far from disintegrating, may be undergoing a kind of structural adaptation to changing economic and social conditions, involving above all a trend to diversification of form. For instance, there are signs of strengthening relationships among wider family networks (nephews, nieces, uncles, grandfathers, etc.); in addition, it has been observed that new forms of familial organisation are emerging in Northern European countries and among the young generation, which are leading to new types of solidarity. While unofficial cohabitation and a high degree of autonomy and mobility are increasingly common phenomena in these relational clusters, the latter are also characterised by greater equity between partners and a sense of responsibility which extends beyond the narrower concept of the institutional family. Statistics from the United Kingdom certainly point in this direction. In 1991, 30 per cent of births took place out of wedlock, compared with less than 12 per cent in 1980. But the proportion of such births registered by both parents rose from half to three-quarters, and more than 50 per cent were registered by parents living at the same address. Against this background it comes as less of a surprise that pan-European opinion polls indicate an increase in all countries over the last decade in the importance people attach to family life.

Finally, especially for those Europeans with the skills and qualifications to establish durable links with the labour market, an extension of the corporate welfare function (particularly in the domains of health and pension benefits) may offer at least a partial alternative to the traditional welfare state. In some respects, such a move would be out of line with the pattern in other OECD regions. After all, in Japan social and economic factors are combining to put considerable pressure on the time-honoured system of lifelong employment and other industry-specific practices and networks which hitherto conferred health and pension rights on employees and acted as an implicit social security net. The United States, for its part, seems to be moving towards universality of coverage for certain welfare benefits. Indeed, the respective European, American and Japanese models of work and welfare provision may, by the beginning of the next century, show an increasing trend towards convergence.

There can be little doubt, however, that the changes sweeping the international economy and transformations taking place within OECD countries will prove a severe challenge to the effectiveness of governance, revealing the state as we know it to be inherently unsuited to its new tasks. With the OECD societies of the future operating much more as networks of people, technologies and communications – unconstrained by highly structured hierarchies and functioning in largely autonomous groups and localities – centralised decision-making in government will become increasingly less effective. At the same time, however, globalisation is likely to continue to exert substantial pressures on nations, regions and local communities to adjust to new economic and social realities. Withstanding such pressures may well surpass the resources and reserves of solidarity available to some of these smaller sub-national entities. Governments will consequently be obliged to find new and more flexible organisational forms and mechanisms for preserving social cohesion and solidarity as the globalisation process unfolds.

The Long-term Outlook for Growth and Employment

by

Emilio Fontela
Professor of Economics
Universities of Madrid and Geneva
Spain/Switzerland

We are suffering, not from the rheumatics of old age, but from the growing-pains of over-rapid changes, from the painfulness of readjustment between one economic period and another. The increase of technical efficiency has been taking place faster than we can deal with the problem of labour absorption; the improvement in the standard of life has been a little too quick; the banking and monetary system of the world has been preventing the rate of interest from falling as fast as equilibrium requires.

J.M. Keynes, *Economic Possibilities for Our Grandchildren*[1]

1. Introduction

Historical evidence indicates that there have been big fluctuations in the rate of unemployment in OECD Member countries. While current rates in Europe and the United States are well above expected levels of frictional unemployment, similar situations could be found before and between the two World Wars. The new features of current trends are:

- Permanently higher unemployment rates: the EC unemployment rate, which stayed at the 2-3 per cent level until the mid-seventies (below the North American 4-6 per cent level of frictional unemployment), has jumped to the 9-11 per cent level during the past ten years (while the North American rate also began fluctuating above previous levels, between 6 and 9 per cent); the number of long-term unemployed is increasing in all countries (with many jobless actually becoming unemployable), and youth unemployment has acquired dramatic characteristics in several countries.[2] Furthermore, "underemployment" in the form of discouraged workers, involuntary part-time work and involuntary early retirement is also

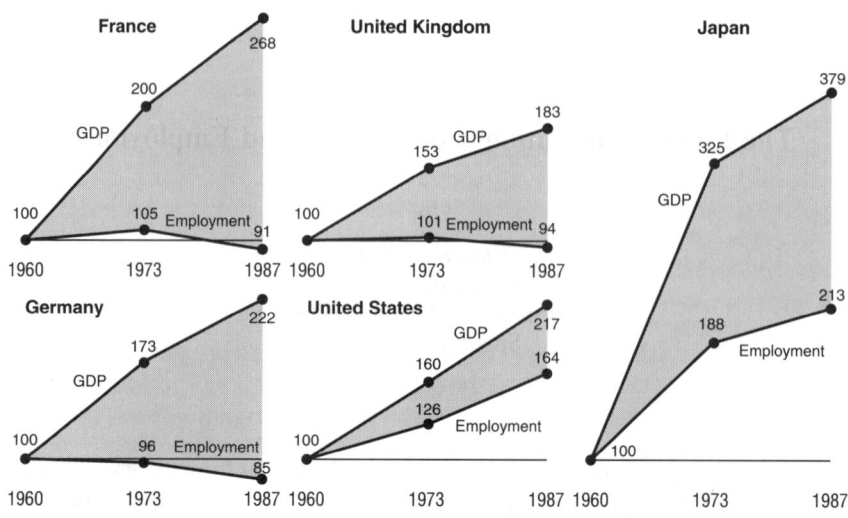

Source: UNDP, 1993.

increasing; in Germany, some projections to the year 2000 estimate official
unemployment at 3.3 million and further underemployment at 2.6 million.
– Lower response of employment to output growth: the elasticity of employment to
output is decreasing (Verdorn's law: increasing output stimulates productivity
growth), and economic recoveries are increasingly de-linked from job creation.
The American and Japanese economies have been less affected by this trend than
the EC countries, many of which are undergoing a process of "jobless growth".[3]
Figure 1 above illustrates that process and the differences observed between
European countries and the United States and Japan.

2. A survey of available long-term employment projections

In exploring the future of employment, thought needs to be given to trends in the
labour force and labour requirements within the structure of productive activities
(employment demand). The study of future equilibrium between employment supply and
demand requires consideration of price mechanisms linked to institutional frameworks
(work legislation, oligopolistic negotiations between social agents, etc.) that are further

subject to change. Matching the socio-economic characteristics of the labour force (age, sex, education, skills, occupations, location, etc.) with the requirements of production systems raises additional difficulties. Most of the available studies offering a long-term outlook for employment deal with only some aspects of this complex system.

Labour force projections

Long-term population projections (up to 2025) prepared by the United Nations, as well as many national demographics studies, provide a basis for computing the possible future size of populations; with fertility rates clearly below replacement levels during the seventies and eighties, all OECD Member countries expect local population declines in the early 21st century (eventually compensated by immigration). When a twenty-year horizon is contemplated – a time frame for which working-age population groups are already born – the main uncertainties concern the evolution of activity rates (labour force participation rates) and migration (de Jouvenel, 1989), and both of these (indeed highly uncertain) key variables are influenced by the level of economic activity, as well as by institutional developments in the area of ongoing education, retirement age and immigration policies.

As to activity rates, the general long-term trends are for an increase or stabilizing in women's rates and a decrease in rates for men above 55 and for young people below 25. The outlook is for progressive stabilization followed by a decline in average activity rates in all OECD countries, beginning (at the latest) in the middle of the next decade (ILO, 1986). In the United States (as in other Member countries), "as the baby-boom generation moves through the years of peak labour force participation, there no longer will be increases in participation due to a large group of people shifting to ages with higher participation. After 2005, with the baby-boom generation moving to ages older than those of peak labour force participation, the tendency will be for the overall labour force participation rate to remain steady or to drop" (Fullerton, 1991).

As to migrations, there is general agreement among experts that OECD countries are likely to receive increasing numbers of immigrants from the rest of the world (developing regions and formerly centrally planned economies), but few experts venture quantitative estimates; available forecasts for the active population are therefore often conservative in this respect. However, in the case of the official US projections by the Bureau of Labor Statistics (BLS), the basic immigration hypothesis figure is 800 000 per year (documented and undocumented); thus, a substantial portion of the expected growth of the labour force, from 125 million in 1990 to 150 million in 2005, is indeed due to immigration.[4]

In Europe and Japan, official population projections are made under the asumption of constant immigration flows, and the result is an expected stability of the labour force by the year 2005.[5] Under present unemployment conditions in Europe, one could even foresee an actual decline of the "local" working population as discouragement keeps a number of potential workers out of the labour force (in particular, women and young people who remain in the educational system), thus leading to lower activity rates;

however, this decline could be corrected if more realistic immigration hypotheses were adopted, *i.e.* at least ones comparable to those used by the BLS for the United States.[6]

A number of available studies show that the future workforce in practically all Member countries will on average become increasingly older, more educated, and move towards occupations requiring higher skills (Johnston, 1991). While the flow of immigrants is generally expected to continue to be mainly unskilled, in western Europe in recent years the immigration of very skilled workers (from eastern Europe) has increased the demand for occupations requiring higher educational attainment.

Employment projections

Employment projections are associated with scenarios of future economic growth and structural change. In recent times the deterioration of economic conditions in the OECD area has led to lower expectations of economic growth, a fact reflected in the available studies of some countries. Thus in the United States, the BLS central employment projection is based on a GNP growth rate of 2.3 per cent a year from 1990 to 2005, compared with a 2.9 per cent rate for the period 1975-90 (Kutscher, 1991). Conventional wisdom among economic forecasters now places the GNP growth rates at between 2.0 and 2.5 per cent for the OECD countries (for the EC, the 2.7 per cent per year projected in 1990 for the period 1990-2010 is today considered ''optimistic''; even for Japan, long-term growth expectations are rapidly declining). The thinking behind this change in expectations could easily be challenged by simple inspection of long-term trends such as the following:

- The increasing amount of resources devoted to industrial R&D should lead to a continuous flow of technological innovations.
- The successful completion of the Uruguay Round of GATT negotiations is likely to stimulate the world trade of goods and services.
- Many developing countries, including China and parts of Latin America, have succeeded in introducing a market-driven high growth process, and other countries in eastern Europe are likely to follow the same path.
- The need to devote unproductive resources to defence expenditures is rapidly decreasing.

Studies conducted in the late eighties were considering trends that did not anticipate any serious long-term unemployment problems. Thus, for the United States, the BLS projections considered that creating 25 million jobs in the fifteen years to come (1990-2005) was a perfectly sustainable proposition; researchers from Prognos considered that in the EC, 10 million jobs would be created during the nineties, thus bringing down the unemployment rate to the frictional level of 6 per cent; the Policy Studies Institute also predicted for the United Kingdom (for the period 1990-2010) that jobs would increase by 3 to 4 million and that there would be a decrease in the unemployment rate.[7] Even more recent projections elaborated in 1992/93 for Germany [by the Institut für Arbeitsmarkt- und Berufsforschung (IAB) in Nürnberg] and the United Kingdom [by the Institute for Employment Research (IER), Warwick University] still considered as most probable a decrease in unemployment before the end of the century. For Germany, a GDP growth rate of 3 per cent per annum from 1992 to 2000 should, according to these projections, bring unemployment below the 2 million level from today's 3.5 million; for the United Kingdom, with a growth rate of 2.1 per cent per annum from 1991 to 2000, unemployment should go down to 2.6 million from its present level of 3 million (DIW, 1990). The only indications of a possible process of jobless growth in the years to come were provided by a prospective analysis of the employment consequences of new technologies [which anticipated a large number of job losses following massive introduction of information technologies (ASSESS Group, 1991)], but the majority of studies from the late eighties neglected the possibility since the available evidence was not really pointing in that direction.[8] Only recently has there been concern about the possibility that employment could increase sufficiently only if GDP growth rates jumped suddenly to "unrealistic" levels (e.g. above 3.5 to 4 per cent per year). This concern has been stimulated by the present economic crisis, with its peculiar mix of cyclic and structural factors (even if the diagnosis of jobless growth can be traced back to the early eighties, the growth performance achieved by OECD countries during the second half of that decade once again changed the perspective of forecasters by 1990, as shown by the projections quoted above).

The future of unemployment: structural factors

It has already been pointed out that the renewed preoccupation with persisting high levels of unemployment in some Member countries is associated with the negative expectations linked to the economic downturn. However, in examining the long term, there may be reasons to believe that structural elements may induce further employment problems in all countries, including those such as Japan and the United States that are still creating many jobs.

Competitiveness and new technologies

The end of the cold war has further stimulated the use of market-driven solutions to economic problems, thus increasing the overall level of competition in a great number of markets traditionally associated with high employment levels (manufacturing as well as services such as telecommunications, transportation or banking). This emphasis on market dynamics has favoured an acceleration of innovation processes based on technologies of the Information Society paradigm (microelectronics-computer-telecommunications) that have a great potential for replacing human labour (automation, robotics, expert systems, etc.). Industries directly associated with the production of capital equipment incorporating these new technologies, or industries using them for their own product innovations, generate new employment; in periods of stagnating demand, however, this positive effect may be less important than the negative impact of labour reduction in production processes.

Firms looking for increased competitiveness have concentrated investment decisions in the area of process innovation, and have opted in many instances for streamlining and externalisation of activities. Employment by large corporations is decreasing as a result, and pressure is put on socio-economic systems to generate more entrepreneurs for an expanding group of small and medium-sized enterprises (SMEs) expected to have the necessary capacity to develop product innovations. Educational and socio-cultural systems are often ill-adapted (particularly in Europe) to cope with this fresh need for entrepreneurial spirit.

It is difficult to know if the innovation process is replacing labour by technologically advanced capital equipment in rigid adherence to the simplest economic logic of cost minimisation (price-comparing capital and labour); nonetheless, it is clear that a new set of strategic considerations and trends heavily influence firms' decisions to reduce total labour requirements:

- "Zero default", the emphasis on quality control, favours the introduction of more reliable production processes and the suppression of the more repetitive jobs (in assembly-belt manufacturing and, progressively, in low-skilled services).
- Miniaturisation and extreme precision, as well as production in controlled environments, going beyond human capabilities.
- Requirements for information accumulation in production processes and for decentralised operations.

The imperative of competitiveness, coupled with the technological revolution, is likely to accelerate the rate of growth of total factor productivity (TFP) – an event long awaited during the seventies and eighties – as well as to increase the rate of capital/labour substitution, leading to a rapid decrease in the total amount of work actually demanded by the productive system.[9]

The productivity of services

While the trend towards increasing TFP and a declining relative need for work have been evident in agriculture for several decades and in manufacturing more recently – the index of employment in manufacturing from 1970 to 1990 has risen in the United States to 105 and in Japan to 108, but has declined in Germany to 86, in France to 81 and in the United Kingdom to 65 – it has often been felt that services, with a lower-than-average level of productivity, could act as the lead sector for job creation in the decades to come. The anticipated changes in the structure of employment from primary to secondary and tertiary sectors have been taking place smoothly in the long run. These trends are evident in the entire OECD area; only countries that have achieved higher competitive positions in manufacturing, allowing them to build up trade surpluses (Japan and Germany), have managed to maintain relatively high levels of employment in the secondary sector. For the United States, the BLS has shown that many manufacturing sectors have already gone beyond the point of peak employment (Bureau of Labor Statistics, 1991).

In the two large OECD countries where total employment is still increasing, the United States and Japan, the growth of employment in services has been higher than total employment growth during the last thirty years, but a progressive de-linking between output and employment in services can be observed, as illustrated by Figures 3 and 4.

Figure 2. **Employment decline comes to manufacturing**
Year of peak employment

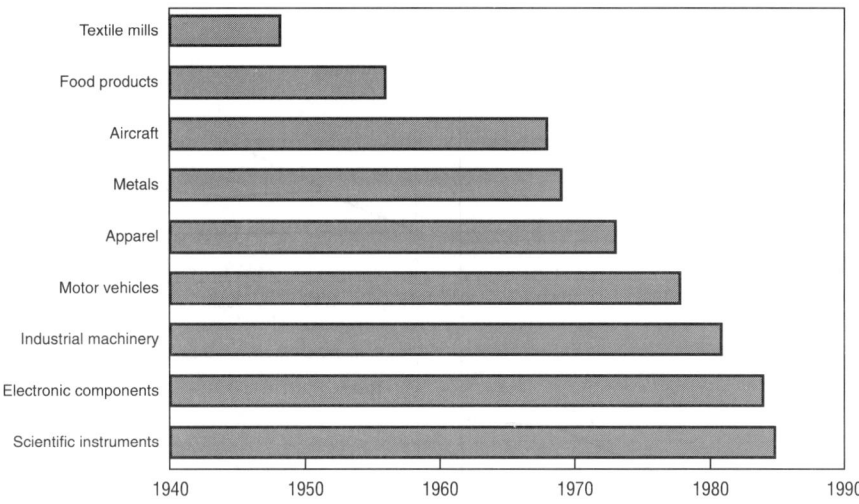

Source: Bureau of Labor Statistics, *Employment, Hours and Earnings,* 1991.

To varying degrees, these trends in structural change have been taken into consideration in some of the more recent employment projections:

- In its central projection to 2005 for the United states, the BLS sees employment in manufacturing of durable goods declining, but 23 million new jobs are expected to be created in service-producing activities (Carey and Franklin, 1991), with 6.1 million in business and health services, 5.1 million in retail trade, 3.2 million in government and 1.4 million in finance and real estate services.
- The Economic Planning Agency of Japan projects an employment decline in the material goods production sector (agriculture, manufacturing and construction) of 2 million workers (from 1985 to 2000); at the same time, employment is expected to grow by 6.8 million in the ''knowledge service production sector'' (management, medical, health, education, leisure, housekeeping, government) and to remain practically stable (+0.3 million) in the ''network services sector'' (energy distribution, transportation, communications, trade, finance, insurance, real estate) (Matsumoto, 1992).

While it is clear that many service activities are not really open to competition (*e.g.* public services), and the stimulus for process innovation is therefore not as strong as in agriculture or in manufacturing, recent institutional trends, as well as government policies

31

Figure 3. **GDP and employment in the United States**

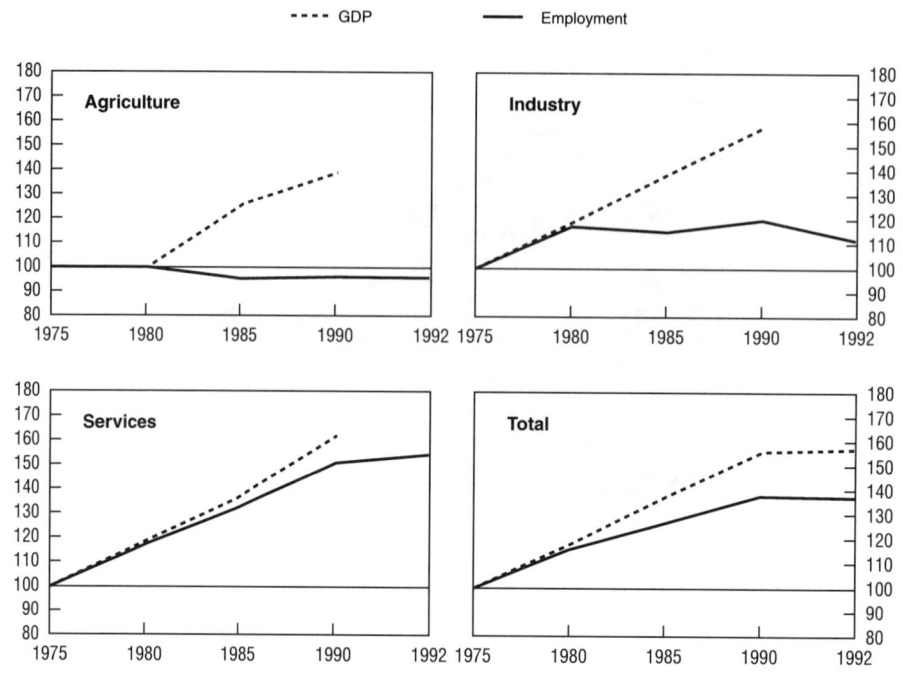

| | Agriculture | | Industry | |
	Employment	GDP	Employment	GDP
1975	100.0	100.0	100.0	100.0
1980	100.7	100.5	115.2	118.3
1985	95.2	125.6	114.2	136.9
1990	96.7	137.9	117.6	154.6
1992	96.4	—	110.4	—

| | Services | | Total | |
	Employment	GDP	Employment	GDP
1975	100.0	100.0	100.0	100.0
1980	116.9	118.0	115.7	117.3
1985	131.7	135.6	124.8	135.1
1990	149.3	160.1	137.4	156.0
1992	152.2	—	137.0	157.4

Source: Michael Hopkins, Background paper for UNDP, 1993.

Figure 4. GDP and employment in Japan

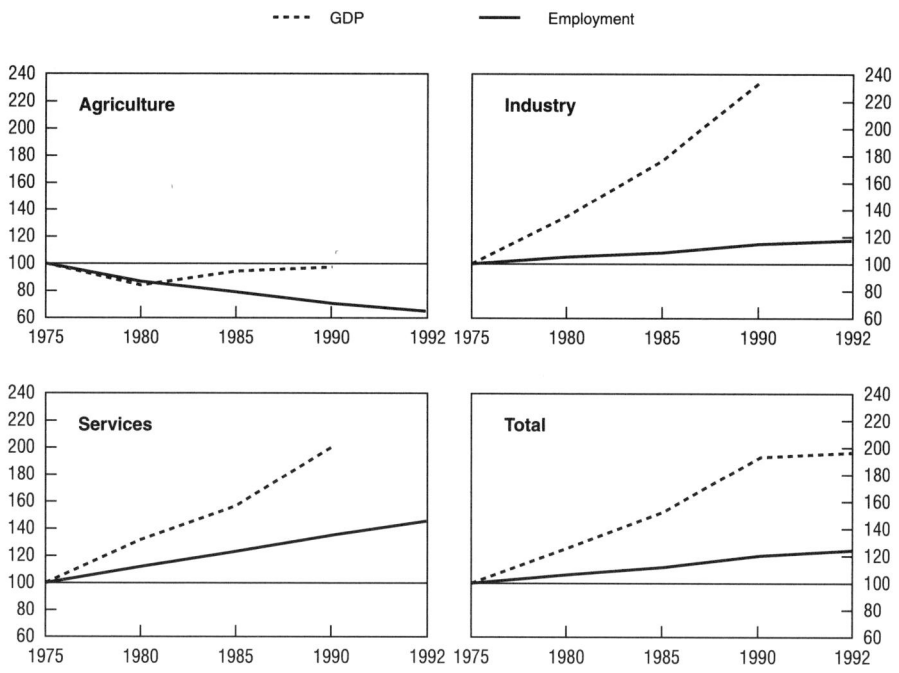

	Agriculture		Industry	
	Employment	GDP	Employment	GDP
1975	100.0	100.0	100.0	100.0
1980	87.3	84.8	104.4	134.7
1985	77.0	94.9	108.1	176.5
1990	68.2	97.4	113.7	232.4
1992	62.2	—	118.9	—

	Services		Total	
	Employment	GDP	Employment	GDP
1975	100.0	100.0	100.0	100.0
1980	111.6	130.4	106.0	125.2
1985	121.7	158.5	111.2	150.3
1990	136.4	196.8	119.6	188.1
1992	141.2	—	123.2	197.3

Source: Michael Hopkins, Background paper for UNDP, 1993.

aiming at deregulation of many monopolistic or highly regulated markets, are favouring the adoption of cost reduction policies in this wide economic sector as well. Among the elements often cited as accounting for a progressive slowdown of employment in services, and even for a future decline in some service activities, are:

- increased foreign competition (as a result of GATT's liberalisation process);
- increased competition due to deregulation or, in the case of the EC, to the introduction of the Single Market for finance, insurance, transport services, etc.;
- demand saturation in sectors reaching maturity; and, obviously,
- the introduction of information technologies.

For the United States, the BLS takes into consideration the fact that some service activities have already reached the point of peak employment (Bureau of Labor Statistics, 1991).[10]

In general, from a methodological point of view, it can easily be argued that most projections directly reflect current events (thus projections made in the late eighties were de facto extrapolating the relatively good employment results of these years), and that they usually neglect the role of macro policy variables in the process of structural change of production and employment.

Figure 5. **Employment decline comes to services**

Year of peak employment

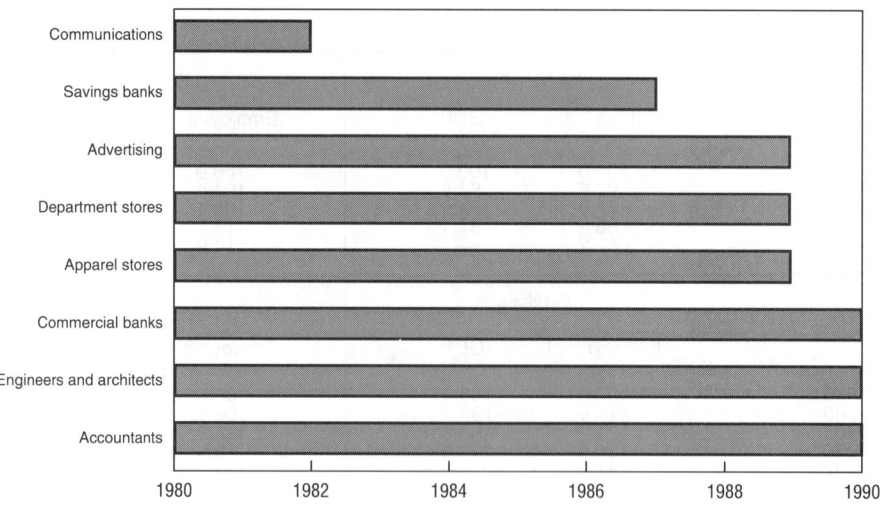

Source: Bureau of Labor Statistics, *Employment, Hours and Earnings,* 1991.

34

The outlook for employment in OECD Member countries described by existing projections does not provide a basis for coherent exploration of the future, but the key unknowns have been identified:

– Immigration to OECD countries is likely to modify existing demographic trends; the active population will probably continue to increase during the next two decades.
– There is certainly a strong cyclical component in present unemployment, particularly in Europe, so that a higher growth rate could considerably alleviate the situation. However, some structural trends indicate more of a long-term problem: most manufacturing and many services (notably network services) have reached or are reaching peak employment and are likely to require less labour in the future.
– Job creation is going to be increasingly concentrated in knowledge-based services, including personal services, and this may require a higher proportion of ''entrepreneurial'' spirit and non-wage-earners, as wage-earners were traditionally concentrated in manufacturing and network services.

3. Main issues in the long-term outlook for employment

The current problem of unemployment in Member countries, the prospects for increasing immigration, the low expectations for economic growth and the mounting evidence that structural change towards services may be reaching its limits all raise many issues as to the future of employment and employment policies. Among these, the following are particularly relevant:

– issues related to the model of structural change;
– issues related to hours of work; and
– issues related to international competition.

The paper does not take up the wider discussion on macroeconomic demand policies; while essential for a full exploration of the future of employment, that topic would require analysis extending beyond the content presented here. The paper also avoids specific discussion on the cost of labour, which is central to the analysis of the employment/unemployment relation and the subject of other OECD publications.

The growth model

Baumol (1967) contemplated the dominant growth model for the future in OECD countries in considering an economy with a high-productivity manufacturing sector and a low-productivity service sector. While a number of network services are likely to join manufacturing at the high-productivity end of the spectrum, many other sectors are and will continue to be closely identified with simple labour-intensive production technologies requiring a very diverse mixture of skills. This model is likely to generate wide divergences in the development of personal incomes, and would require substantial amounts of income redistribution to maintain social cohesion.

The contemplation of a future with growing income inequalities requiring income redistribution forces one to look for a more adequate system to encourage employment while at the same time avoiding excessive losses of human assets (creativity, pride, self-esteem, etc.). Proposals in respect of minimum guaranteed income, or of negative taxation for low-income households, may be more stimulating for the proper functioning of the labour market (*e.g.* in a context of complementarity between education and work) than the present system of unemployment benefits (Friedman and Friedman, 1980).

The existence of a large low-productivity sector (including public administration), assisted by redistribution processes (through income redistribution or through prices), forces the high-productivity sector to maintain an ongoing fight for productivity improvements, which probably cannot be sustained over the very long term. Some studies show that societies are reaching a point where the main competitive capacity of a high-productivity sector will indeed be determined by the performance of its complementary low-productivity sector: inefficient trade, collective services and public administration constitute real handicaps for the other competitive activities.[11] A new growth model is required, one which would introduce high-productivity gains into traditionally low-productivity sectors.

Economic growth depends on the progress of total factor productivity. Empirical studies show clearly that the bulk of total productivity gains during the fifties and sixties is accounted for by the productivity of intermediate products, equipment goods and durable goods, the core of the manufacturing sector. From there, productivity gains spread to the rest of the industrial sectors and finally to the consumers through declines in the relative prices of manufactured goods. As these declines were encouraging further demand, the process produced many virtuous circles and granted practically full employment.

During the long period of slowdown in the seventies, new investment in manufacturing was naturally devoted to rationalisation rather than to expansion, introducing a process of substitution of labour by capital equipment (often with relatively small gains in total productivity) and leaving to the rest of the economy the task of employing a growing labour force. Faced with a somewhat similar situation, both the United States and Japan have maintained high levels of employment by expanding a low-productivity, low-wage tertiary sector, thus accepting in fact the duality of a high-productivity sector producing traded goods and a low-productivity sector producing non-traded goods and services. These differences in productivity growth were partly reflected in relative prices (redistribution through prices).

In Europe, the welfare state kept high entrance conditions for new employment (particularly in terms of minimum wage and the cost of social security), thus creating a different kind of dualism by accepting the development of an ''underground'' production system unwilling to follow official labour practices. It has also increased employment in the public sector, and thus accorded that sector undue weight in the national income.

Potential gains of TFP in manufacturing are now smaller as the main economies of scale have been attained, the institutional opening of markets has achieved its main objectives, and there are additional environmental constraints. Assuming it unlikely that OECD countries will simply return to the postwar growth model, the only reasonable alternative is to develop a model based on total productivity gains in the service sector.

In this model, productivity gains in intermediate (business) services will spread to the other industrial sectors through decreases in relative prices (reversing a major long-term trend), and those in private and public consumer services will encourage additional demand in an expansionary process similar to the one observed in the past for manufacturing products. The potential demand for personal services is very high (needs like education, health or leisure are far from saturation), and a decrease in their relative price should rapidly increase effective demand.

If the Member countries are unable to develop this new model of growth, the only valid alternative to full employment is "dualistic", one in which the low-productivity sector is centred on final demand activities (not providing inputs to the high-productivity sector) and in which these activities are highly price-inelastic – thus operating in a cultural context that accepts a high relative price for human-intensive services as a proof of service quality. The model of full employment then becomes a cultural issue with many delicate "social traps".[12]

Working hours

Historical evidence shows that the hours of employment per person are continuously decreasing, with shorter weeks, longer holidays, early retirement and delayed entry into the workforce.[13] This is part of the gain of labour productivity. There is also some evidence that the total amount of hours of employed work required by complex production systems is decreasing. Should the decrease in the hours of work of each individual be accelerated? Is it simply an arithmetic problem? Is the problem of growing structural unemployment simply one of imperfect distribution of working hours in an economy? The issue has stimulated a number of ingenious proposals in many OECD countries to redistribute employment with little or no effect upon labour costs.[14]

Part-time employment is spreading rapidly in all Member countries, a development stimulated both by demand factors (there are an increasing number of jobs that do not require long hours of presence, or can be performed with great flexibility) and by supply factors (e.g. women dividing their time between their job and family activities).[15] This trend will probably continue into the future and will be increasingly associated with the use of new information technologies (tele-working, work measured by tasks performed rather than by time spent).

Also the growth of self-employment can be associated with a de-linking of working time from work schedules and labour contracts. Self-employment and micro-enterprises are growing (and are expected to continue to grow) in all OECD countries, these being factors which increase the work flexibility required by firms that are "externalising" many activities (related to services in particular).[16]

Employment projections should probably take into account the advent of a system in which the labour contracts originating after the Industrial Revolution and progressively standardized by the welfare state will cover only a small part of the jobs performed by an active population using its available time very differently.

In a long-term perspective, consideration should be given to a time usage model showing continuous complementarity between education and work, with very smooth transitions both for younger and older generations. Figure 6 illustrates this concept, adding the elements of leisure and family; the complementarity remains smooth throughout the entire life cycle. The current educational system in OECD countries is, for the moment, poorly adapted to this long-term evolution (the ''permanent education'' concept is still in a very early stage of development, and its operational instruments in the production system are scarce); two possible points of departure for the new lifetime model are the reduction of working weeks and the introduction of sabbatical periods.

As public administration is the largest single employer in all OECD countries, it is a likely candidate to lead the way with a new model of development involving high productivity in services. In line with this, one would also expect public administrations to be leaders in the introduction of new technologies or of new forms of work (reduced and flexible time schedules, part-time jobs, temporary jobs, jobs complemented with permanent education, sabbatical leave, etc.).

Figure 6. **Complementarity of work, education, leisure and family life throughout the life cycle**

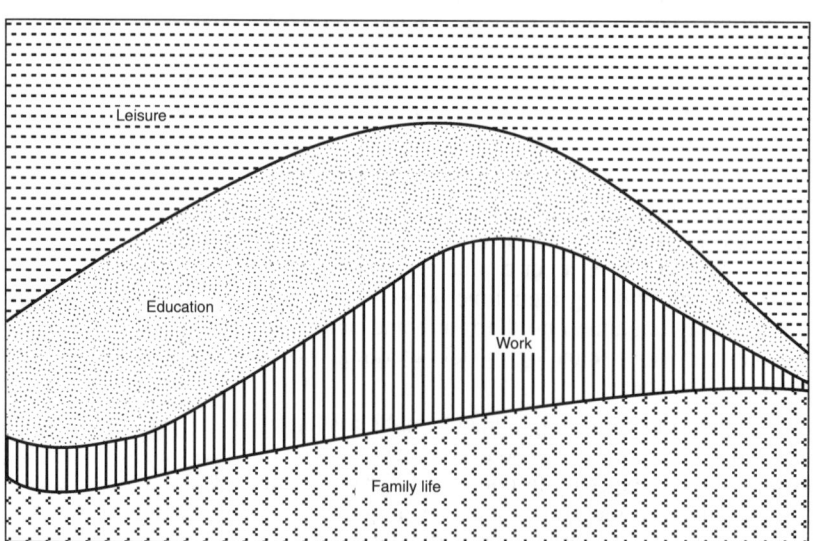

Source: Emilio Fontela, *España en la década de los ochenta,* Presidencia del Gobierno, Madrid, 1980.

International competition

In all OECD countries, there is a direct conceptual association between employment and competitiveness; thus for many analysts, the high unemployment levels in Europe are a result of market losses to imports from other OECD areas (for products with a high technology content) and from nonmember countries (for products with a low technology content). Using the argument of employment in a framework of lost competitiveness, some analysts go so far as to propose protectionistic measures (mainly for sensitive imports from nonmember countries).

If, as often stated, a model that increases productivity faster allows a country to become more competitive, one could hardly expect from such an evolution a real long-term solution to the unemployment problem, as it would only be a transfer of unemployment to another, less competitive trade partner.

It should be noted also that the international relative position of unit labour costs in OECD countries is heavily affected by exchange rates and that the departure from purchasing power parity rates observed during the last few years has, in some cases of overvalued currencies, been an important factor behind the loss of competitiveness, market share and employment. In an open and integrated international market, the parameters defining the cost of labour are increasingly complex.

Furthermore, Member countries have a global trade surplus with nonmember countries, and it is likely that for most of the OECD area, the amount of job destruction originating from imports of ''sensitive'' products is negligible (if often politically important). In a framework of increasing globalisation, nonmember countries have an obvious role to play in low-skill, labour-intensive activities; OECD protectionism could only slow down a normal process of economic optimisation at world level.

That same logic of competitiveness has been used to fashion arguments relating to the cost of social welfare that point to existing differences between Europe, other OECD areas and the rest of the world. Such differences have very much to do with the mechanisms for financing social welfare. There are probably financing (tax) systems that are more successful than others in enhancing employment, but few studies are available on this subject. (Those that are show that taxes which increase the relative cost of labour are indeed detrimental to the development of employment.)

4. Final considerations

Within the OECD, the employment problem is concentrated in Europe and has a strong short-term content; as during the period 1985-90, an economic recovery could solve the more critical situations. However, even assuming a return to a ''normal'' growth path (around 3 per cent GDP annually), there is sufficient evidence to show that employment demand in the OECD will slow down further or even decline (if, as expected, network services start reducing their demands). The long-term outlook indicates that it will be increasingly difficult for all Member economies to achieve full employment under satisfactory social conditions (that is, avoiding precarious or informal employment); the final answers that will be provided by the economic and social systems are still unclear, but in all circumstances they imply deep structural changes.

A new growth model reducing the relative prices of intermediate and final-demand personal services in order to have them better meet growing existing needs is not yet foreseen in the medium term; an acceleration of the reduction of working time could take place thanks to new forms of labour agreement (part-time, temporary jobs, etc.), but these are not yet culturally accepted; the same applies to possible radical changes in the lifelong relation between education, work and leisure. Nevertheless, these three types of structural changes are increasingly necessary.

The extrapolation of current models offers rather unsatisfactory scenarios: some simply rely on a coexistence of normal workers with a growing segregated group of unemployed and underemployed; others establish full employment by increasing the level of precarious employment and low-paid jobs. All these scenarios are dualistic in essence and could give rise to social conflicts. Policies are urgently needed in the OECD countries to limit the extent of these dualistic processes and to move towards a new model of structural change.

Notes

1. Reprint of 1930 edition, EntroCon. A similar essay was first presented in 1928 as a talk at Cambridge's Political Economy Club.

2. By the end of 1994, according to OECD projections, the jobless total will have risen to 23 million in the EC, 8.25 million in the United States and 1.7 million in Japan; unemployment in the OECD could reach 36 million workers or 8.7 per cent of the active population.

3. The following table is extracted from P. Omerod (1993), "Notes on Unemployment", Henley, quoted by A. Hingle, "Note on a New Model of Development", DG XII/A/3, EC, September 1993.

**Growth of economy and employment in the European Community countries
and in the United States**

(1970-92, percentages)

	Growth of economy (real terms)	Growth of employment
Germany	70	8
France	75	7
Italy	84	8
United Kingdom	52	3
Spain	93	–2
United States	76	45
EEC	73	7

4. Fullerton (1991) notes: "Under the assumption of lower net immigration that characterizes the middle population projection, the labour force would be 147 million, 3.2 million fewer than under the high net immigration scenario BLS decided to use. The difference in workers between the two projections is solely due to immigrants."

5. The Eurostat projection for a constant European labour force is extracted from de Jouvenel (1989) and Japanese projections are from ILO (1986).

6. Lesourne (1986) pointed out that even in a "low profile" scenario, one should add to an expected EC population of 312 million in 2025 some 25 million immigrants, an increase which soars to 65 million in a more extreme scenario.

7. The OECD Future Studies Information Base (OECD International Futures Programme) includes several publications related to these projections, including Prognos AG (1990), *Entwicklung des Arbeitsmarktes in der Gemeinschaft,* Basel, and the Policy Studies Institute (1991), *Britain in 2010,* London.

8. Nadel (1993) reports on the most recent projections prepared by the IAB and the IER.

9. For a comprehensive analysis of the economic consequences of technological change as well as of the past evolution of sectorial total factor productivity, its economic causes and its consequences, see OECD (1992) and the basic computations by Englander and Mittelstadt (1988).

10. It should be added that Schmid (1993) considers that in the United States employment is likely to decline during the nineties in insurance, banks and security brokerage, and to remain constant in retail and wholesale trade, restaurants and advertising – areas in which the BLS is still expecting additional job creation. Similar doubts concerning the BLS projections were raised by du Granrut (1992).

11. Alessi, Fontela and Lo Cascio (1989), using an econometric model with a core set of input-output relations, have tested several scenarios of sectorial productivity change, showing that increasing productivity in the "protected" sectors of the Italian economy reduces direct employment but also, by way of increased competitiveness, induces indirect employment and has in the end a more positive employment effect than a corresponding productivity effort centred only on the "exposed" sectors.

12. The potential dangers of the "dualistic" model were outlined by Gershuny (1985) in two long-term scenarios:
    – the Servant Economy, with a rapid development of a "servant" class working in low-productivity services, with lower salaries and precarious employment conditions;
    – the National Opera Service ("the Albanian State Opera Company, whose apparently execrable performances are played to a house filled, not by the bourgeois voluntarist process of subscription, but rather on the socialist principle of conscription, of workers from local factories") resulting from massive inefficient employment in the public sector.

13. While a century ago a worker used to spend some 3 000 hours per year for his employed activity, this total has decreased to some 1 700 hours today in Europe – thus at an annual average rate of –0.6 per cent. During the sixties and seventies this rate increased (to about –0.8 per cent a year), but during the eighties the average number of hours worked per year stabilized and even increased in some OECD countries. For a detailed analysis of trends and international comparison, see Marchand (1992) and Boulin (1992).

14. The debate on the reduction of hours of work is particularly heated in France. Already in 1979, econometric studies performed by INSEE (Oudiz *et al.,* 1979) were showing that a reduction of one hour in the average working week totally compensated by a corresponding wage decrease could create in three years some 250 000 jobs. In the studies conducted for the preparation of the XIth Plan (1993-97), the Chariman of the Group on Employment, B. Brunhes (1993), after observing that the average working week had decreased 20 minutes a year between 1950 and 1982 and had remained stable thereafter, recommends steps to introduce new reductions.

15. Part-time jobs are an increasing share of total jobs; ILO has conducted studies of this evolution showing that in OECD countries, the percentage of women in part-time jobs is on average of the order of 70-80 per cent. Part-time jobs play very different roles in different national labour markets:

Part-time jobs in 1990

(as percentage of total employment)

Netherlands	31
Denmark	26
Sweden	25
United Kingdom	24
United States	21
Australia	20
Canada	15
Germany	13
France	12

Source: ILO, Eurostat.

For the United States, this trend is further analysed in Tilly (1991).

16. In the BLS projections for the United States, the non-farm self-employed, having grown from 6.2 million in 1975 to 9 million in 1990, are expected to reach 10.8 million by 2005. In the United Kingdom, according to IER, independent employment grew from 2.1 to 3.1 million from 1981 to 1991, and is expected to reach 3.4 million in 2000.

Bibliography

ALESSI, M., FONTELA, E. and LO CASCIO, M. (1989), *Occupazione 2000: Tra modernizzazione e nuovi dualismi,* Assolombarda, Milan.

ASSESS Group (1991), "The Social and Economic Implications of New Technologies", EC-DG XII - FAST-MONITOR, Report D 10, Brussels, November.

BAUMOL, W.J. (1967), "Macroeconomics of Unbalanced Growth: The Anatomy of Urban Crisis", *American Economic Review,* Vol. 57.

BOULIN, J.-Y. (1992), "L'évolution du temps de travail en Europe", *Futuribles,* Paris, April.

BRUNHES, B. (1993), "Choisir l'emploi", *Futuribles,* Paris, February.

BUREAU OF LABOR STATISTICS (1991), *Employment, Hours and Earnings.*

CAREY, M.L. and FRANKLIN, J.C. (1991), "Industry Output and Job Growth Continues Slow into Next Century", *Monthly Labor Review,* November.

DIW (1990), *Neue Technologien und Beschäftigungsstruktur,* Berlin.

ENGLANDER, S. and MITTELSTADT, A. (1988), "Total Factor Productivity: Macroeconomic and Structural Aspects of the Slowdown", *OECD Economic Studies,* No. 10.

FRIEDMAN, Milton and FRIEDMAN, Rose (1980), *Free to Choose: A Personal Statement,* Harcourt Brace & Company, New York.

FULLERTON, H.N. (1991), "Outlook: 1990-2005, Labour Force Projections: The Baby-boom Moves On", *Monthly Labor Review,* November.

GERSHUNY, J. (1985), *The Future of Service Employment,* University of Bath.

GRANRUT, Charles du (1992), "L'emploi tertiaire aux États-Unis: La fin de l'âge d'or?", *Futuribles,* July.

ILO – International Labour Office (1986), "Economically Active Population Estimates and Projections 1950-2025", *World Summary,* Vol. V, Geneva.

JOHNSTON, W.B. (1991), "Global Work Force 2000: The New World Labor Market", *Harvard Business Review,* March-April.

JOUVENEL, Hugues de (1989), *Europe's Ageing Population: Trends and Challenges to 2025, Futures* and *Futuribles,* co-publication.

KUTSCHER, R.E. (1991), "Outlook: 1990-2005. New BLS Projections: Findings and Implications", *Monthly Labor Review,* November.

LESOURNE, J. (1986), "The Immigration Issue", *Futures,* 18-6.

MARCHAND, O. (1992), "Une comparaison internationale des temps de travail", *Futuribles,* Paris, May-June.

MATSUMOTO, K. (1992), "The Future of the Service Industry in Japan", *Japanese Economic Studies,* Vol. 20, No. 4.

NADEL, H. (1993), "Les prévisions d'emploi en Allemagne et au Royaume-Uni", *Futuribles,* Paris, October.

OECD (1992), *Technology and the Economy* (TEP Report), Paris.

OUDIZ, G., RAOUL, E. and STERDYNIAK, H. (1979), "Réduire la durée du travail: quelles conséquences?", *Economie et Statistique,* 111, May.

SCHMID, G. (1993), "Services with Fewer Workers", *1993 Ten-Year Forecast,* Institute for the Future.

TILLY, C. (1991), "Reasons for the Continuing Growth of Part-time Employment", *Monthly Labor Review,* March.

UNDP – United Nations Development Programme (1993), *Human Development Report 1993,* Oxford University Press, New York.

Workforce 2005: The Future of Jobs in the United States and Europe

Alan Reynolds
Director of Economic Research, Hudson Institute
United States

Herman Kahn, the founder of the Hudson Institute, was often involved in questioning the seemingly endless stream of dismal forecasts. Technological optimism became a hallmark of the Institute's work, emphasizing the ability of intelligent and creative people to produce a brighter future. This tradition has continued with the work of Julian Simon on the implausibility of running out of raw materials; that of Dennis Avery on the feasibility of feeding a growing world population; and that of George Gilder on the exciting prospects of new technologies of information and entertainment.

In 1987 the Hudson Institute published a bestseller, *Workforce 2000,* written by William Johnston and Arnold Packer and sponsored by the US Department of Labor. This study too had an optimistic slant, proposing educational and economic reforms that could lead to unprecedented economic progress in the United States and the world. Yet what continue to attract the most attention are the sections on potential problems, rather than solutions. Indeed, many of the concerns raised in *Workforce 2000* have now become conventional wisdom. Much has changed, however, since 1987; some of the data that were fresh then are now a decade old, and need re-examining.

This paper is divided into six sections. It begins by looking at where past projections of US employment and the ageing of the population have gone wrong, and where current projections are likely to go wrong. The second section deals with the "education gap" – updating a key concern of *Workforce 2000,* that the jobs of the future will require lengthy schooling and high skills, while the labour force will supposedly become less educated and less skilled. The third deals with the notion that shifting employment from goods to services will either depress real earnings or make them less equal. The fourth section disputes some common misperceptions regarding an alleged secular decline in US productivity and real earnings in the recent past. The fifth weighs the costs and benefits of an ageing population, in the United States and elsewhere. The sixth section deals primarily with Europe, and the growing belief that chronic unemployment is aggravated by productivity improvements and could be helped by a shorter working week and early retirement. The paper concludes with some comments on the importance of improving incentives for human capital accumulation among younger people, and for older people to work and save enough to avoid being overly dependent on the generosity of younger taxpayers.

1. Projections of US employment and demographics: past and present

As recently as 1989, Bureau of the Census estimates of the "dependency ratio" (the ratio of children and older people to the working-age population) showed an increase from 62 to 67 for the year 2020. By 1992, though, this had been revised to show no increase at all. Meanwhile, the 1989 estimate of a dependency ratio of 78 by the year 2050 has since been lowered to 69 (see Table 3 below).

The 1985 Bureau of Labor Statistics (BLS)'s mid-range ("moderate") estimate of US employment in 1990 turned out to be too low by 6.4 million jobs (4.7 per cent) by one measure, despite a recession at the time of the Gulf War. The actual number of jobs in 1990 exceed by 3 per cent the "high" estimate made in 1985. That same year, the size of the 1990 labour force was also underestimated by 3 million, and GDP per employee was underestimated by 2.9 per cent (Saunders, 1992, Table 2, p. 18). Over longer periods, the cumulative effect of such errors can become quite substantial. The 1978 estimate of US merchandise exports in 1990, for example, was 31 per cent below the actual figure.

Changes of this magnitude over rather short periods should produce a healthy scepticism regarding the accuracy of the latest forecasts about demographics or employment in the distant future. One obvious reason for the tendency to underestimate future employment is that projections based on past trends cannot possibly account for entirely new products and services that are being created at a hectic pace. One can only guess about future jobs in biotechnology, new materials, new sources of energy or new communications, transportation or entertainment technologies.

The BLS offers three scenarios based on annual growth rates of real GDP of 1.5, 2.2 and 3 per cent from 1992 to 2005; the three range from dismal to cautious. The "high" growth path is simply the postwar average (GDP growth from 1983 to 1993 was nearly 2.9 per cent); the "low" 1.5 per cent growth rate would be unprecedented over such an extended period. Real GDP from 1929 to 1940 averaged 2.2 per cent a year, for example, which is similar to the BLS's moderate forecast (Bureau of the Census, 1975, Table F31, p. 226). Yet that period was called "the Great Depression".

The central or moderate projection yields a 1.5 per cent annual increase in employment through 2005, down from 2.3 per cent from 1975 to 1990. Total civilian employment in this scenario is thus projected to increase by 24.5 million by 2005, or 1.8 million per year. The main constraint is not in the demand for labour but in its assumed supply. The labour force is assumed to grow by only 1.3 per cent a year, down from 1.7 per cent in the 1979-89 period, so that unemployment falls to 5.5 per cent even with very moderate economic growth of 2.2 per cent a year. Despite the relative shortage of labour, real capital per employee rises by only 5.4 per cent from 1992 to 2005, compared with 17.4 per cent from 1979 to 1992.

Although the moderate projection will be used in this paper, the so-called high projection, with 8 million *more* jobs, seems more plausible.

A breakdown of the BLS moderate employment projection by broad occupational categories is shown in Table 1. These categories are somewhat arbitrary, and cover a wider range of incomes than the median weekly earnings may suggest. Administrative support includes such different occupations as records processing and insurance claims adjusters. "Technicians" lumps aircraft pilots together with computer programmers. "Precision production, craft and repair" counts auto mechanics along with electricians and computer repairmen. "Marketing and sales" mixes cashiers with stockbrokers and real estate agents. "Agriculture" shows employment gains in forestry and gardening slightly outnumbering a loss of unskilled farm labour.

"Professional specialty" occupations show a doubling in the numbers of engineers, scientists and computer systems analysts, to 1.5 million. Larger absolute gains are projected for teachers, librarians and counsellors (from 5.9 million to 8 million). "Professionals" also includes writers and entertainers, a group with an extremely wide variation in earnings.

Table 1. **BLS projections of the increase in US employment, 1992-2005**

Occupational group	Median weekly earnings, males, 1992 (dollars)[1]	Total employment in 2005 (millions)	Number of jobs added (millions)	Percentage change
Services	330	25.8	6.5	33.4
Professional specialty	770	22.8	6.2	37.4
Executive, administrative and managerial	784	15.2	3.1	25.9
Administrative support, including clerical	482	25.4	3.1	13.7
Marketing and sales	523	15.6	2.7	20.6
Precision production, craft and repair	503	15.3	1.8	13.3
Operators, fabricators and labourers	393	17.9	1.5	9.5
Technicians and related support	591	5.6	1.4	32.2
Agriculture, forestry, fishing and related jobs	269	3.7	*	3.4

* = 120 000.
1.   For full-time or equivalent workers.
Source: Silvestri, 1993; weekly earnings from Bureau of the Census, 1993, Table 671.

In the service category, there are some well-paid chefs and cosmetologists, and skilled workers in health services and law enforcement. Curiously, the BLS projects a decline in private household workers (from 869 000 to 583 000), although increased female participation rates and the rise in the number of very old people surely suggest strong demand for better-trained and certified day care and adult care specialists.

Even "Operators, fabricators and labourers", as well as farming, includes people who operate increasingly sophisticated machinery. There are relatively few US jobs, now or in the future, that are unambiguously in the "low skill" category – 85 000 parking lot attendants in 2005, 180 000 service station attendants, 142 000 taxi drivers. In fact, some arduous jobs that require little skill (such as 134 000 refuse collectors) often command surprisingly high wages. This is likely to be even more true in the future, as a larger proportion of relatively affluent older people bid for fewer strong young people to do strenuous or time-consuming chores.

Many analysts have looked at these broad categories of employment, or even at the division of employment between manufacturing and services, and concluded that future job opportunities will be bleak for the less educated or skilled. This conclusion cannot be based solely on the categories in which "new jobs" are likely to be created, however, because many of those now employed in "old jobs" will have to be replaced as the baby boomers begin to retire. In all plausible scenarios, the growth of overall employment exceeds the growth of the labour force, creating a tight market for labour in general and particularly for increasingly scarce workers in their twenties.

A related source of worry has less to do with the quantity of low-skilled jobs *per se* than with a supposedly more rapid increase in the supply of workers seeking those jobs. The problem, according to some observers, is that the quality of a large segment of the US labour force has been declining and can be expected to decline further in the future.

2. Education, ethnicity and immigration: will US workers be up to the job?

One of the concerns first raised in *Workforce 2000* was that a large portion of the workforce of the future might be inadequately schooled/trained for the more complex jobs.

A source of confusion about the demand for less-educated workers may be cleared up simply by differentiating percentage increases and absolute numbers of jobs. The projections in Table 1 show large percentage gains for professionals, managers and technicians. However, they also show larger absolute numbers of jobs that do not necessarily require many years of formal schooling, such as service, clerical and sales workers. The largest absolute gains in employment – with 408 000 to 786 000 new jobs apiece – are for cashiers, clerks, truck drivers, waiters, orderlies, retail sales and food preparation workers. The only highly skilled occupations with comparable gains are nurses, systems analysts and teachers.

With the apparent exception of services (where weekly wages can be misleading, due to wide variation and increasingly short working weeks), those occupations showing the smallest absolute job gains, such as farm workers and labourers, also had the lowest weekly wages in 1992. That relatively low-paying jobs cannot compete in the labour market with better-paying jobs is neither a new development nor something to be feared. The same is true of the continuing shift from arduous manual labour toward services, which is the whole point of inventing machines to replace muscles.

A minor theme of *Workforce 2000,* expressed on fewer than three pages, may have received more attention than was warranted – namely, that a majority of the new entrants to the labour force will be minorities and immigrants who currently have, on average, fewer years of schooling. The BLS now estimates that Blacks and Hispanics will make up 34.8 per cent of the new entrants to the US labour force from 1992 to 2005. At the end of that period, though, those two groups will still only account for 22 per cent of the total labour force, compared with 18.8 per cent in 1992. Some popular writers have added immigration to the total, but that involved double-counting (since many immigrants are Hispanic, Black or both).[1]

Workforce 2000 identified several possible problems with the changing ethnic composition of the workforce (Johnston and Packer, 1987, pp. 89-91). One was the decline in Black and Hispanic male labour force participation in the seventies. If that had continued, though, it would mean that there would be fewer minority males in the labour force, so their job skills would be irrelevant. In any case, the decline became insignificant in the eighties. Labour force participation among Black males was 70.3 per cent in 1980 and 70.1 per cent in 1990. Among Hispanic males, it was 81.4 per cent in 1980 and 81.2 per cent in 1990 (Bureau of the Census, 1993, Table 622). The BLS now projects higher participation rates among minority males, partly because more of them will be of prime working age (25-55). That is one reason why Blacks and Hispanics will constitute a slightly larger share of the labour force.

A more important concern voiced in *Workforce 2000* was the relatively low levels of schooling among minorities in 1983. However, the past is not the future. The least-educated members of the labour force are relatively old, so most of them will be retired by 2005. Among the 33.1 million persons over age 25 who had not finished high school in 1990, 70.7 per cent were over the age of 45 and 56.2 per cent were older than 55 (Bureau of the Census, 1993, Table 234). Some researchers count high school graduates starting with age 18, but that is misleading because many people are still in high school at that age. Moreover, some who drop out return later, or finish high school while in military service. In 1986, for example, only 64.9 per cent of Blacks aged 18 or 19 had finished high school, but 81 per cent of those aged 20 to 24 had done so (Kutscher, 1989, Table 3, p. 71). In 1991, 14.2 per cent of Blacks and 13.4 per cent of Hispanics aged 18 to 21 were still in high school, while 28.3 per cent of Blacks and 23.9 per cent of Hispanics in this age group were enrolled in college. From 1989 to 1991, the average high school dropout rate among males was 3.9 per cent for Whites, 5.5 per cent for Blacks, and 8.9 per cent for Hispanics (Bureau of the Census, 1993, Tables 261 and 263). Comparable figures for 1980 were 6.4 per cent for Whites, 8 per cent for Blacks and 16.9 per cent for Hispanics.

The average years of schooling have been rising quite rapidly among Blacks, and somewhat less so among Hispanics (many of whom are recent immigrants). Among Blacks over the age of 25, 67.7 per cent had finished high school by 1992, compared with only 31.4 per cent in 1970. By 1992, 20.1 per cent of Blacks had completed 1 to 3 years of college, and an additional 11.9 per cent had completed 4 years. In 1970, only 4.4 per cent had finished college. Among Hispanics over age 25, 51.3 per cent had finished high school by 1991 and 9.7 per cent had finished college, compared with 32.1 per cent and 4.5 per cent, respectively, in 1970 (Bureau of the Census, 1993, Tables 49 and 233). Of those taking SAT tests for college entry, 10.4 per cent were Black in 1992, compared with 7.9 per cent in 1975. "Between 1976 and 1991... Black students' SAT verbal scores increased by 19 points and mathematics scores increased by 31 points". Verbal and math scores for Mexican-American students also rose 7 points and 17 points, respectively, while scores for Whites declined (US Department of Education, 1992, pp. 54 and 227). The quality of minority schooling has improved even before college. Reading proficiency scores for 17-year-old students show a gain from 243 to 267 among Blacks between 1979-80 and 1989-90, and from 261 to 275 for Hispanics. In math, Black scores rose from 268 to 289 from 1977-78 to 1989-90, and Hispanic scores from 276 to 284 (Bureau of the Census, 1993, Tables 265-267).[2]

Clearly, the next generation of Black and Hispanic workers will be much better educated, on average, than the current generation, as the less-schooled older workers retire.

There may, however, be a growing mismatch between unschooled workers and more difficult jobs for Hispanics, particularly new immigrants. Hispanics are projected to account for 11 per cent of the labour force by 2005, up from 8 per cent in 1992, while the percentage of Blacks in the labour force rises insignificantly, from 10.8 to 11 per cent. Neither change is nearly as significant as the fact that the overall labour force will be older. Yet Hispanics (particularly those from Mexico and Puerto Rico) do face unique problems.[3] Immigration already accounted for about 23 per cent of the growth of the labour force from 1981 to 1989, up from 12 per cent in 1971 to 1980 (Borjas, 1993a, p. 485). Since Hispanics accounted for a sizeable share of immigration, what is often thought of as a problem of poor schooling for native minorities is, to a large extent, really a matter of attracting less-educated immigrants. Minorities, including the children of immigrants, are rapidly improving their schooling, but new adult immigrants are arriving in the United States with a lower stock of human capital.

George Borjas (1993b, pp. 9-11) reports that "in 1980, only 13 per cent of high-school dropouts were foreign-born; by 1988 immigration made up over 25 per cent of workers with less than a high school education... In 1960, newly admitted immigrant men (that is, immigrants who had been in the country less than five years) had 0.4 more years of schooling and earned about 13 per cent less than native men. By 1990, newly admitted immigrants had 1.4 fewer years of schooling and earned 38 per cent less than natives".

Table 2 shows the percentages of Hispanics now employed in some of the key occupational groups shown in Table 1. Clearly, Hispanic workers are heavily represented among categories that are expected to add few jobs – agriculture and operators, fabricators and labourers. Hispanics are also heavily represented in the less-skilled services, where jobs will still be abundant but compensation is likely to remain relatively low.

The declining educational achievement of recent immigrants has more to do with different incentives in tax and transfer policies than with any changes in immigration

Table 2. **Employment of full-time workers 16 years and older, 1992**

(percentages)

	Non-Hispanics	Hispanics
Managerial and professional specialty	27.6	13.5
Technical, sales and administrative support	31.8	24.8
Service occupations	13.1	20.2
Precision production, craft and repair	11.0	13.4
Operators, fabricators and labourers	13.7	22.3
Farming, forestry and fishing	2.7	5.9

Source: Cattan, 1993, Table 5, p. 11.

policy (which has no effect on Puerto Rican or illegal Mexican immigrants). Countries such as Mexico and the Asian NICs became acutely aware of the high cost of "brain drain" in the late eighties, and therefore sharply reduced their highest marginal tax rates. In Mexico, for example, the highest personal income tax rate was reduced from 55 to 35 per cent as the US federal tax was being increased from 28 to 40 per cent (plus state income taxes of up to 11 per cent). The highest effective tax rates in most Asian NICs now rarely exceed 30 per cent, even at very high incomes. Such policies help retain the best educated and most skilled, talented and industrious workers. Mexico has stopped exporting so many physicians and engineers to the United States.

On the other hand, as Borjas remarks, "the United States now taxes the most able and subsidizes the least productive. Economic conditions in the United States...[have] become a magnet for [foreign] workers with relatively low earnings capabilities". This is a problem, but not one that could not be fixed. Upgrading the quality of future immigrants would require more restrictive policies about eligibility for public support among new immigrants, more competitive tax rates at higher incomes, and perhaps some schooling, skill or asset requirements as a condition for legal immigration.

The increasing scarcity of youth

Although much has been written about the ageing of the labour force (a subject discussed below), less attention has been paid to the impending scarcity of younger workers. BLS estimates show the number of men aged 25 to 34 declining by nearly 2.9 million from 1992 to 2005, or 14.7 per cent. The number of women in this age group also declines by more than 900 000, or 5.8 per cent. Even broadening the age group to 25-44, there will still be a drop in the male labour supply of 1.4 million. Aside from teenagers, younger workers – particularly young men – are going to become increasingly scarce. Moreover, teenagers who are in the full-time, full-year labour force are obviously not attending college, which still leaves the country with fewer young college-educated people.

The relative scarcity of workers of post-college age casts considerable doubt on the political theme that the next generation of young people are going to have a hard time earning as much as their parents. Unlike the situation that faced the baby boom generation, particularly those who graduated from college in the seventies, there will be no surge of young people seeking jobs, thus depressing starting salaries. And there will be no subsequent surge of young couples trying to buy housing, which helped bid up living costs.

If older workers were perfect substitutes for the young, women perfect substitutes for men and high school graduates perfect substitutes for college graduates, the falling supply of men in their twenties and early thirties would present no difficulties. Yet there are some occupations typically held by young men which have great difficulty attracting either female or older workers – skilled construction trades and the repair of increasingly complex automobiles and aircraft, for example. As these examples illustrate, it is not always feasible to substitute either machinery or imports for labour services that require some heavy lifting. Teenagers might be trained to do some of these chores, but that will require more accessible vocational training or apprenticeships, and employers are not apt to make such risky investments in training if faced with a high minimum wage or high government-mandated benefits or severance pay.

While it has become almost obligatory to worry about a future shortage of intellectual power, it is at least equally likely that there will be a shortage of muscle power. This is only one reason to question the common assertion that unskilled and semi-skilled labour will fare poorly in the coming decades. Another is that older people with higher incomes become less willing to do arduous or time-consuming work themselves, such as mowing the lawn, fixing the plumbing or painting their own houses. Since there will be many more people growing old, this must raise the demand for a wide variety of household maintenance and repair services, thus bidding up relative wages in such occupations. The demands of older, more affluent people will also contribute to the already amazing proliferation of global restaurant chains, as well as movie theatres and shopping centres. Those in their forties and fifties may save a larger fraction of their incomes, but their incomes are so much higher than those of the young that they will nonetheless constitute an enormous market – particularly for services.

Speculation about a shortage of jobs for the least skilled appears unwarranted. There will be ample growth in employment for the rapidly shrinking numbers of US citizens who lack high school or vocational training. There would be a serious shortage of people to do unskilled work were it not for immigration, which may reach a million per year. Most of the relatively unskilled jobs added in the future will be in services, but that is nothing new. The service jobs that are created will far outnumber the jobs that still remain to be lost in unskilled farm and factory work. In addition, those new service jobs will pay higher wages for less onerous work. For those not satisfied with such work, there will be many more opportunities to upgrade skills; computer stores, for example, are now selling training lessons, as well as training videos and software.

Ironically, those who fret about insufficient employment opportunities for a shrinking number of high school dropouts are matched by others who express anxieties about recent and future college graduates, who are said to face increasingly difficult competition that will force them into low-paid work. A recent article in *The Futurist* (1993), "Too Many Graduates, Too Few Jobs", paraphrases a BLS study in suggesting that college graduates in the 1990s and early 2000s will face more competition for jobs than their counterparts in the eighties. What the BLS actually forecast, in a paper published in July 1992, was that the growth of positions "requiring" a college degree would slow to 2.5 per cent a year between 1990 and 2005, down from 4.1 per cent in 1984-90 (Shelly, 1992, pp. 13-21). This is largely because the BLS also forecast a slowdown of jobs in general, to 1.3 per cent a year if the 1990-91 recession is included. For the demand for college graduates to rise twice as fast as overall employment does not sound like much of a crisis. The comparison with 1984-90 is misleading, since that period involved a rapid recovery from a deep and prolonged recession in 1980-82.

In late 1989, the BLS was still forecasting "a significant easing of the competition for jobs that has characterized the job market for college graduates since the early 1970s" (Kutscher, 1989, p. 70). This earlier projection remains the most likely outcome. In the seventies, a huge increase in the number of baby boomers aged 25-34 in the labour force created a highly competitive market for new college graduates, and as a result the financial returns to higher education fell. That was considered a serious problem at the time, because of the reduced incentive to invest time and tuition in a college education. In the eighties, the growth of college graduates slowed sharply for demographic reasons, and the returns to higher education improved. However, this too is now considered a serious problem, because income gaps widened between those with and without a college degree. Americans are hard to please.

The shift toward a pessimistic outlook with regard to opportunities for college graduates between 1989 and 1992 probably just reflected the cyclical weakening of the economy in that period. Even in the recession of 1990-91, though, mean average earnings among college graduates aged 21 to 29 were actually 18.7 per cent higher than in 1987-89, and the percentage of those accepting "low-wage" jobs (defined as those paying too little to support a family of four) remained near one-third (Ryscavage, 1991, Table 7, p. 24). Because US employment growth is almost certain to exceed labour force growth in the next two decades – particularly for those nearing the usual age of college graduation – the returns to college education will remain quite attractive, at least on a pre-tax basis. There is some evidence that the recent increase in US marginal tax rates, if kept in place, will reduce personal investment in human capital (Trostel, 1993). In that case, though, the relative scarcity of highly educated people should eventually bid up the pre-tax salaries they are offered, leaving after-tax incomes about the same in the long run.

Young Americans, both college-trained and not, are likely to receive rapid increases in real incomes in the next two decades, and salary premiums for the increasingly plentiful middle-aged workers will meanwhile be smaller than in the recent past. The age-income profile will be somewhat tilted in favour of scarce younger workers and against abundant older workers, though lifetime incomes will rise substantially.

3. Is a service economy something to fear?

The concern about a shortage of employment for those with less schooling or training arises in part from an assertion that those who did not complete high school in the past would have been employed at relatively generous wages in the manufacturing industries. Such "good jobs" in blue collar assembly work are said to be vanishing because of increased competition from labour-rich countries such as China, India and Mexico. This is said to force unskilled workers into lower-paying service jobs.

It is a romantic illusion that blue collar factory work is inherently more desirable or more lucrative than white collar service work. In reality, those with neither a high school education nor a vocational skill have not been able to compete for the dwindling number of better-paid manufacturing jobs for many years. Instead, they have worked in low-wage sweatshops, picked fruit and vegetables, mowed lawns, driven taxis, worked as labourers on construction jobs or as janitors, and so on.

Unskilled workers have always been heavily represented in service industries – house-cleaning, bussing tables, lawn-mowing, and the like. What has changed is the rising quality of those jobs. People who used to operate elevators have been replaced by electric buttons, people who used to carry luggage have been replaced by luggage with wheels, people who used to hand you a towel in the rest room have been replaced by towel dispensers and hand dryers, bank cashiers have been replaced by automated tellers, household cooks have been replaced by restaurant chains and microwave ovens. Jobs such as movie ushers or help to carry groceries were killed by the minimum wage. There will be abundant opportunities for relatively unskilled workers in the service industries of the future, but these will involve mostly indoor work with no heavy lifting. Service workers will be using more high technology, but such technology will be increasingly user-friendly (*e.g.* bar-codes for cashiers and diagnostic machines for auto mechanics).

Manufacturing has accounted for a declining share of employment for many decades, in almost all major economies. This is a natural consequence of mechanisation and related productivity increases, comparable to what happened earlier in farming. The percentage of US non-farm payroll employment accounted for by manufacturing fell from 33 per cent in 1950 to 23.4 per cent in 1979, though the absolute number of manufacturing jobs nonetheless rose by 5.8 million in that period. The percentage then dropped to 16 per cent by October 1993, with a loss of 2.5 million manufacturing jobs since the 1979 peak (US Bureau of Labor Statistics, 1992, Table B-1, p. 45). The BLS projects only a slight job decline through 2005, when manufacturing will account for only 13.2 per cent of all non-farm employment. This may well prove to be optimistic, but also somewhat misleading. Services that were once conducted within oversized manufacturing firms (such as public relations, accounting, law and economics) are being increasingly contracted to outside specialists. Nonetheless, Tom Peters notes [in his "Foreword" to Quinn, 1992 (p. ix)] that "75 to 95 per cent of a 'manufacturing' firm's employees are in non-manufacturing activities – engineering, design, sales, marketing, information systems, purchasing, service, distribution". Since a sizeable share of such service jobs will go to outside firms in the future, it would not be surprising to see fewer than 10 per cent of US jobs classified as manufacturing by the year 2005.

The decline in US employment within "manufacturing" firms certainly does not suggest "deindustrialisation". The manufacturing component of the industrial production index (where 1987 = 100) rose from 78.8 in 1980 to 112 in September 1993 – an increase of more than 42 per cent – and this phenomenon of increasing manufacturing output while reducing employment is not unique to the United States. From 1970 to 1985, manufacturing jobs as a share of total employment fell from 22.7 per cent to 17.2 per cent in the United States, but also from 27.2 per cent to 21.7 per cent in the OECD area as a whole (Dollar and Wolff, 1990, Table 5.8, p. 109). The OECD's larger share of employment in "goods" production, compared with services, simply reflects lower productivity in comparison with the United States in agriculture, construction and manufacturing.

US workers are not simply being pushed out of manufacturing jobs. They are being lured by superior income growth in other sectors. From 1980 to 1992, average hourly wages in manufacturing rose from $7.27 to $11.46, or 57.6 per cent. In the same period, wage rates rose 80.3 per cent in services (from $5.85 to $10.55), 63.6 per cent in wholesale trade (from $6.96 to $11.39), and 86.9 per cent in finance, insurance and real estate (from $5.79 to $10.82).

The fact that wages have risen far more rapidly in services than in manufacturing is not widely known, and was not anticipated in *Workforce 2000*. The study noted that wages are less equally distributed in service industries, but that simply follows from the fact that such diverse jobs are classified as services. With over 70 per cent of US employees directly employed in services, and another 20 per cent performing service jobs within manufacturing firms, the dispersion of incomes is necessarily large. It does not follow that reducing manufacturing's share of jobs from 16 per cent today to 13.2 per cent in 2005 will have much effect on "inequality". Ageing of the workforce will have much more impact, for the obvious reason that older workers typically earn more (and produce more) than inexperienced young people. The wider dispersion of annual incomes as a result of ageing may trouble egalitarian scholars, but it does not imply that lifetime earnings will be less equal. As young people grow older, they too will earn more.

The authors of *Workforce 2000* warned that "the problem is not so much the inequality of service industry wages as it is the slow growth of those wages and their diversion to pay for pensions and medical bills" (Johnston and Packer, 1987, p. 30). Since then, however, service wages have grown much faster than manufacturing wages, and increasingly generous tax-free pension and medical benefits have become a larger portion of compensation in (particularly unionised) manufacturing as well as services.

Padráig Flynn, Commissioner for Social Affairs and Employment at the European Commission, recently wrote (1993, p. 38) that "we need to revitalize the manufacturing industry to slow the decline in male employment. The importance of a healthy manufacturing sector cannot be overemphasized". Yet the US manufacturing sector is quite "healthy", and becoming more so as employment declines, specialisation of services increases, and output per worker rises. Men are quite capable of working in nonmanufacturing jobs, and the vast majority are already doing so.

Politicians' efforts to "save jobs" are typically focused on low-wage declining industries. Much of the US debate about NAFTA, for example, concerned trying to keep Americans working in the broom industry, or sewing low-cost clothing, or picking tomatoes (Reynolds, 1993). Such jobs are doomed anyway, because consumers do not value the product sufficiently to justify a competitive wage. Either consumers substitute more easily mechanised products (plastic brooms and drinking glasses; corn sweetener for sugar), or producers substitute machinery (textiles, agriculture). Efforts to "save jobs", however, keep resources tied up in the losers while depressing real incomes in the growing sectors through tariffs and other subsidies to the declining industries. Rapidly growing economies continuously move the workforce out of relatively primitive activities toward more sophisticated products and services. In doing so, as Robert Lucas observes, they accumulate human capital "through the high learning rates associated with new activities, and through the spillover of this experience to the production of still newer goods" (1992, p. 267).

The quaint notion that goods are somehow superior to services is rapidly becoming as archaic as the idea that we must subsidise and protect agriculture to keep more people on the farm. A handful of visionaries have grasped the critical role of knowledge workers in the 21st century. In a new book of vital significance, *Intelligent Enterprise*, James Brian Quinn (1992, pp. 415-416) demonstrates in great detail that "services and the management of intellect will be the keys to future economic success for nations – as well as for all businesses regardless of whether they are in the 'manufacturing' or 'service' industries... Effective services actually create new markets for manufactured goods, lower costs for manufacturers, and are central in increasing the value-added for almost all manufacturers". Peter Drucker (1992, pp. 12-14) likewise suggests that the country that first succeeds in raising the productivity of knowledge and service work will be the dominant economy of the next century.

The federal training lobby

Assertions that future job opportunities are likely to exceed the capabilities of an increasingly uneducated US labour force are not consistent with the evidence, with the relatively minor exception of immigrants. However, the theme of an undertrained labour force is nonetheless quite popular among interest groups seeking larger government subsidies for education and training (including politically powerful teachers' unions). The National Association of Temporary Services, which may not be a disinterested source, funded a study which claimed that 75 per cent of all US workers will need to be retrained by the year 2000 (Secco, 1992, pp. 30-32). There is a sense in which that might be correct, but it does not follow that taxpayer-financed or subsidised "training programmes" are likely to meet this need in a cost-effective manner.

There is no question that the pace of technological change has been and will remain quite challenging. Learning must be a continuous process, not an event that ends with the receipt of some credentials. However, the relevant sorts of education are not confined to classrooms or equivalent formal training programmes. Many people continually have to master new computer software, for example. At the same time, though, on-line data bases, CD-ROMs and interactive multimedia are rapidly bringing unprecedented access to information in an extremely time-effective way. Indeed, as Lew Perlman (1992) forcefully argues, traditional classrooms and degrees are becoming almost obsolete.

With the exception of specialised professions and skilled trades, most formal schooling mainly provides people with the language and math skills needed to acquire job-specific training later, on the job. Most "on-the-job training" is informal, consisting of learning-by-doing. The National Longitudinal Survey of Youth, which has tracked a cohort of young people annually since 1979, found that 38 per cent of those aged 21-29 had received some sort of explicit job training from 1986 to 1991. That mainly consisted of company training (23.7 per cent) and seminars outside of work (11 per cent), which are usually financed partly or entirely by employers. Fewer than 5 per cent had received training from vocational and technical institutes, and fewer than 2 per cent apiece from apprenticeships or correspondence courses. Employer training programmes were either more available to or more utilised by college graduates (35.3 per cent) than high school graduates (19.4 per cent).

Since the 1960s, more than fifty federal training programmes have been launched in the United States, with results that ranged from ineffective to corrupt (*e.g.* the infamous $53 billion Comprehensive Employment and Training Act) (McKenzie, 1988, pp. 198-199). The rationale for such government intervention is that employers may underinvest in training because they cannot be sure that trained employees will not move to another firm. However, employees themselves have ample incentive to invest time and money in their own training, if that training is effective in increasing their prospective incomes. Because effective job training yields a large private benefit to the trainee – as well as spillover benefits to society – the case for taxpayer subsidies for training (as opposed to, say, student loans) is far from self-evident. Only ineffective training requires the bribery of subsidies, and this is precisely the sort of training that government programmes are most likely to offer. Indeed, government programmes may displace more effective efforts that would otherwise be conducted by potential employees and employers.

There is no justification for the presumption that even the training and job placement of the least qualified workers can best be handled by government agencies, or even by nonprofit agencies. A new for-profit business called "America Works" has had great success in New York City, and has just begun in Indianapolis. This company concentrates on a very brief period of basic training on how to get and keep a job, rather than starting with a lengthy period of formal classroom teaching. It recruits people currently on welfare and actively markets those people to business, providing any necessary support services (such as day care) to minimise absenteeism. The jobs must pay more than minimum wage and provide health benefits. If the new employees are hired after a 4-6 month trial period, the government then pays the company a fee which is much smaller than the cost of keeping people on welfare. In New York City the retention rate is said to be 85 per cent, and the average person placed had previously been on welfare for five years.

The underlying premise of government training programmes is that public officials can somehow predict which jobs will be available in which locations, the types of skills those jobs will require, and any future shortage or surplus of potential employees applying for those positions at the wage and benefit level that will be offered. To believe that this is possible involves what Hayek called the "fatal conceit" of central planning. In reality, bureaucrats have neither the omniscience nor the incentive to match needed skills

59

with available workers. The same holds true for the educators being funded by such programmes, who would naturally prefer to teach those subjects in which they have acquired some expertise. No one knows better what new skills a worker can best utilise than the worker himself.

The most effective way to encourage personal investment in human capital is to empower individuals. Human capital depreciates to zero at death or retirement, the points at which investments in schooling or training cease to yield any return. Unlike investments in physical capital, though, investments in human capital are not generally tax-deductible. Such investments are not treated as a cost of production, but as consumption (even in national income accounts). This biased tax treatment is particularly punitive toward upgrading skills in middle age, since there are fewer years left to recover the return in higher annual incomes. Some educational expenses may be deductible in the United States, but only after graduation and only under the perverse condition that such training must not be designed to make a person qualified for a better job.

The absence of depreciation or expensing for human capital means the tax system would be skewed against such investments even if income from labour were taxed at the same rate as income from, say, stocks or housing. Yet the US tax system, like those in most other countries, imposes steeper tax rates on the returns from human capital than on those from physical capital. On the one hand, investments in human capital are not subject to the 28 per cent federal tax on capital gains, as most other investments are (housing is a partial exception). If a new engineering degree raises a worker's market value over time, he or she is only taxed on the resulting income, not on the appreciation itself. However, this benefit is more than offset by the rising rate and base of the social security tax, which exempts all return from non-human capital. This disparity is even greater in Europe, where social security taxes are higher and capital gains taxes usually lower than in the United States.

A simple solution would be to permit qualified educational and training expenses to be written off over the years remaining before normal retirement (*e.g.* over forty years for a 25-year-old graduate student). By increasing the individual's demand for human capital, such depreciation allowances would create new human capital industries that cater to the highly specific needs of different individuals and age groups. Employers would also be encouraged to offer relevant training, because workers would be more willing to share the cost, as they should.

4. Did the United States gain jobs by lowering living standards?

US employment has doubled since 1960, while employment in the European Community increased by only 10 per cent (*The Economist,* 1993). From 1972 to 1991, the average growth of employment in the United States was 2 per cent a year, compared with 0.5 per cent for the four largest European economies [*OECD Economic Outlook,* 1992 (December), Table R17, p. 217]. Despite some adjustment problems from contracting the defence industries, there is no sign that "the American job machine" is slowing down. US civilian employment increased by 21.6 million between December 1982 and October 1993 – a 2.5 per cent annual rate of increase from 1982 through 1989, followed by a loss of 1.1 million jobs between December 1989 and December 1991. By October 1993, the year-to-year increase was back to 1.9 per cent. BLS projections of a mere 1.5 per cent rate of increase through 2005 are clearly quite conservative, and limited by the supply of US workers rather than by the likely demand.

Europeans are often advised to take solace in the belief that the rapid employment growth of the United States was a consequence of low productivity and wages. Richard Freeman (1988, p. 298) writes that "the United States has paid for job creation with slow growth in real wages and productivity". British economists Andrew Glyn and Bob Rowthorn (1988, pp. 194-199) claim "the ability of the United States to keep employment expanding reflects the fact that US productivity growth has slowed down".[4] A recent article in the *OECD Observer* (1993) says, "in the United States strong employment growth over the last decade has gone hand-in-hand with a fall in real wages for the lowest paid workers. This has given rise to concerns over whether improved job performance can be bought only at wages which risk creating a class of working poor".

Such "stylised facts" require closer examination.

First of all, the notion that real wages have fallen for two decades in the United States is a result of excluding all benefits; dividing weekly wages by 40 hours to measure hourly wage rates; excluding the rapidly increasing proportion of salaried and self-employed workers; using a year (1973) in which price controls understated inflation as the base year; and adjusting for inflation by using the discredited pre-1983 consumer price index (which understates real wage gains through 1983 by exaggerating inflation).

It is certainly true that the US economy suffered real income losses during the stagflationary episodes of 1974-75 and 1978-80. A US Department of Labor report (1992, p. 8) notes that "during 1978-80 there was a dramatic fall in wages and salaries adjusted for inflation...Beginning in 1982, this pattern was reversed, with wages rising more rapidly than prices". What is suspicious is that the real wage declines of 1978-80 are so often attributed to the period after 1982, which is when the big employment gain occurred. The Clinton Administration's initial budget plan, "Agenda for Change", even defined "the eighties" as starting in 1977.

The previously cited comment from the *OECD Observer* about the "fall in wages for lowest paid workers" is particularly affected by bad timing, since that decline occurred entirely from 1978 to 1982 (mostly in 1980), not "hand in hand" with the subsequent surge of employment. The claim of Barry Bluestone and Bennett Harrison, in *The Deindustrialization of America,* that the growth of US jobs in the eighties largely consisted of low-wage service jobs is logically inconsistent with their corollary theme that such low-wage workers fared particularly badly. As Gary Burtless observes, "If employers were creating a disproportionate number of jobs that required few skills and little education...[then] the wages of less skilled workers would be bid up relative to those received by better skilled, more educated workers" (1990, p. 7). This is the opposite of what happened. Returns to higher education rose in the eighties, despite a sharp slow-down in the annual flow of new high school graduates and dropouts into the labour market.[5]

Real disposable income per capita, in 1987 dollars, rose from $12 154 in the fourth quarter of 1982 to $14 324 in the third quarter of 1993 – an increase of 17.9 per cent. Real per capita personal consumption (living standards) rose 22 per cent in the same period, reflecting sizeable wealth gains and unreported income (US Council of Economic Advisers, 1993, p. 6). Since labour income accounts for an overwhelmingly large share of total income, how could such large gains in income and consumption be consistent with a secular decline in real wages?

In reality, hourly wages and benefits, measured in 1992 dollars, rose from $9.83 in 1970 to $12.01 in 1992 – a real increase of 22.2 per cent (*Economic Report of the President,* 1993, Table B-42, p. 396). It is true, as noted earlier, that wage gains in manufacturing trailed behind those in services. It is also true that benefits have been a rising share of compensation, because these have become more generous to a larger proportion of workers (*e.g.* defined contribution pension plans and insurance for drugs, dental care and mental health). Figures on "family" income also did not rise quite as rapidly as income per worker, due to a rapid decline in family size (some figures count young and retired one-person households as families) and to a rapid increase in the proportion of families that consist of a young non-working mother with children and no spouse. "The declining proportion of married couple households and rising proportions of single parent families and nonfamily households", notes a Census Bureau study, "had a large negative impact on the nation's median income level" (Ryscavage *et al.*, 1992, p. 19). The breakdown of paternal responsibility is indeed a major social problem in the United States, but the change in family structure is often confused with weak income growth among the same sorts of families compared over time. Median income does not show what happened to some typical or representative families over the past decade or two, but instead refers to very different definitions of families at different points in time.

Actually, the increase in real hourly compensation in the United States was larger than the measured 22 per cent between 1970 and 1992, due to surveys that exaggerate actual hours worked. Measured weekly hours fell from 38.8 in 1965 to 34.4 in 1992 – but people often misreport, say, an increasingly common "9 to 5" schedule (35 hours) as 40 hours. As Juster and Stafford have shown, "reports of market work continue to be overrepresented by numbers like '40' even when actual hours on the job continue to decline". By examining records of actual hours worked, Juster and Stafford conclude that "there has been a simultaneous understatement of both the rise in real wages and the decline in work hours because hourly wages are typically computed by dividing annual or weekly earnings by an increasingly overstated work hours figure" (1991, pp. 493-494).

Another study by Grubb and Wilson (1992, p. 25) finds that the increasing variety of work hours between voluntary part-timers and those who work overtime or at two jobs is the main source of measured inequality of wages: "increasing inequality in hours worked has more than offset greater equality in wage rates". Those who sought part-time work in the eighties, such as students and young mothers, were able to find employment.[6] If they had instead remained unemployed, they would not have been included in the average wage statistics, and weekly or annual wage figures (which are sometimes improperly used to estimate hourly wages) would not have been diluted by the inclusion of millions more part-time workers.

There is no credible evidence of a secular decline in US living standards, particularly since 1980. Even if there had been a decline in typical US incomes, it would be quite implausible to blame that on increased international competition, as some economists have done. As a matter of theory, that would imply that more competition and freer trade make economies less efficient and thus reduce average productivity – which would entail discarding every economics textbook since Adam Smith. As a matter of fact, those who have investigated widening disparities between high-skilled and low-skilled workers have discovered that same phenomenon in nearly all industrial countries – including Germany and others with large trade surpluses.[7] Moreover, blaming increased gaps in incomes on trade cannot explain "the increased inequality within specific industries, especially in those industries that have little connection to international trade" (Danziger and Gottschalk, 1993, p. 11). There was, for example, a particularly large widening of income differences in US management and sales.[8] There are many plausible explanations of why it pays to stay in school or work longer hours, but the increased volume or competitiveness of international trade is not one of them (Bound and Johnson, 1992).

The so-called "vanishing middle class" is yet another conventional confusion. The percentage of US families earning more than $50 000 a year, in 1991 dollars, rose from 27.3 per cent in 1980 to 33.8 per cent in 1989, with a matching reduction in the percentage of "middle class" families earning from $15 000 to $50 000. It is not that "the rich got richer", but that a larger percentage of families did so.

What about the alleged slowdown in US productivity growth? The measure usually cited is output per hour for the non-farm business sector (which shows how little respect Americans accord agriculture). On an index where 1982 = 100, non-farm productivity rose from 87.6 in 1968 to 99 in 1980, or a bit less than 1.1 per cent a year. By 1992, the index was up to 115.6, or 1.4 per cent a year. Once again, a problem of the seventies continues to be blamed on the eighties.[9] However, there is reason to believe that US productivity gains in the eighties have been seriously underestimated by the inclusion of financial services.

From 1979 to 1988, there was an estimated annual productivity gain of 4.9 per cent in communications and 2.7 per cent in wholesale trade, belying the common notion that productivity gains are small in services. However, estimated productivity supposedly fell by 0.4 per cent a year in finance, insurance and real estate – a sector with unusually strong wage gains (Quinn, 1992, p. 13). Why would employers bid up wages in a sector in which labour was not adding value? Why did investors likewise bid up the values of financial stocks?

The financial sector obviously suffered some unique disturbances in the eighties, including the failures of many banks and thrifts, overbuilding and loan defaults in commercial real estate, large casualty losses in insurance due to natural disasters, and a shake-out of some big investment companies. Still, there were enormous improvements in the breadth, speed and quality of financial services that are almost surely being neglected in the productivity figures. Automated teller machines, computerised securities trading, mortgage-backed securities and mutual funds are obvious examples.

As Figure 1 shows, the productivity of nonfinancial corporations (1982 = 100) rose from 86.9 in 1965 to 97.4 in 1980 – less than 0.8 per cent per year. However, nonfinan-

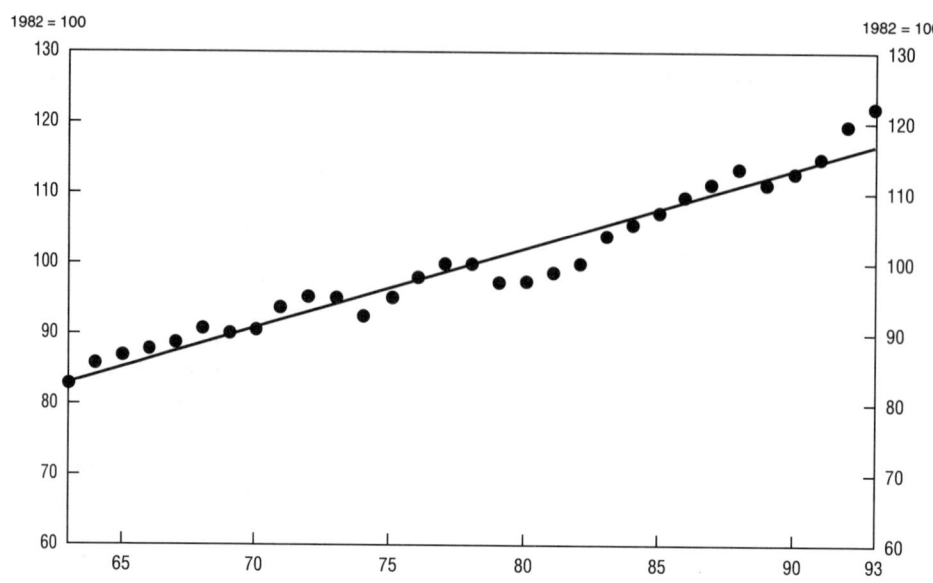

Figure 1. **Productivity of US non-financial corporations**

Trend line: 1963-93. 1993 projected from first half.

cial productivity subsequently rose to 119.4 in 1992, or 2 per cent per year. The gain in 1993 was at least 2 per cent. Far from slowing in the eighties, the rate of increase in the productivity of nonfinancial corporations has more than doubled.

If there was any productivity slowdown since 1980, it had to be in the relatively trivial noncorporate sector, finance or government. Productivity of government services, like finance, is also estimated to have fallen by about 0.4 per cent a year. However, government productivity is quite impossible to measure because one cannot know the value of services that are not sold. This makes international comparisons of GDP per worker a poor proxy for business productivity, because government services account for a significantly larger share of GDP in Europe than in the United States or Japan. Productivity of government services may have increased more or less than the statisticians estimate, but the question itself has little to do with "competitiveness" because government services are, unfortunately, not easy to export. Moreover, any "per worker" comparison over time, whether of GDP or investment, is likely to make Europe look artificially strong, because there has been so little growth of private employment.

The likely mismeasurement of productivity in services means GDP figures are also misleading, particularly for purposes of international comparison. National figures on the percentage of employment accounted for by services are suspiciously similar to the percentage of value-added (GDP) supposedly accounted for by services. This surely reflects statistical convenience rather than reality. Because it is so difficult to measure the value and quality of service output, such output is often assumed to be proportional to (or a bit less than) the labour input: hire more government workers, and GDP appears to rise.

In the OECD statistics, for example, services accounted for 58.9 per cent of Japanese employment in 1991, and 55.7 per cent of GDP. In the United States, services supposedly accounted for only 68.8 per cent of GDP, but 71.8 per cent of employment (*OECD In Figures,* 1993, pp. 26-27). The difference between the United States and Japan is particularly implausible for finance, insurance and real estate. In those activities, Japan supposedly produces 16.4 per cent of its GDP with only 4.8 per cent of employment, while the United States supposedly produces only 25.1 per cent of GDP with 14.6 per cent of employment (pp. 34-37). As with Japanese investment statistics, the supposedly lofty level of productivity in ''finance, insurance and real estate'' may involve miscounting the inflated cost of real estate as real output. Whatever the source of such confusion, the fact is that detailed productivity comparisons by the McKinsey Global Institute, as well as Japanese sources, show Japanese productivity in retailing and most other services to be less than half the productivity levels of the United States (Baily, Bator, Solow *et al.,* 1992).[10] This means the portion of Japan's GDP accounted for by services must be much smaller than the proportion of employment, or the US portion of GDP accounted for by services must be much larger. Both countries cannot possibly have roughly equivalent proportions of GDP and employment in the service sector if US service productivity is twice as large. The GDP figures must be either seriously overestimating both the level of real output and overall productivity growth in Japan, or grossly underestimating such figures for the United States.

Japan is not nearly as close to catching up to the United States as is commonly supposed. The United States is simply undervaluing its services. Similar problems contaminate the world's archaic, merchandise-based trade data. Since US service exports are not generally subject to duties, and are often made by small enterprises (aside from airline travel), they are almost surely undercounted. As Dollar and Wolff (1990, p. 189) point out, ''some of the leading sectors in terms of exports are university education; amusements; medical services; communications; financial services; business services; and computer software''. It is difficult to believe that every US video tape, CD, software programme and computer database used outside the United States is properly recorded as an export, much less every foreigner using US universities, hospitals or economic consulting services. Official estimates show a US trade surplus of about $60 billion in services, but the true figure could easily be twice that large. And the faster the world moves toward a service economy, the more serious such measurement problems become.

Entertainment is already the second largest US export after aerospace, and is sure to become much larger with the rise of interactive multimedia and virtual reality (Kiechel, 1993). Yet Americans are inclined to be more concerned with where blank video tapes and CDs are manufactured, rather than who puts the value-added on them. They still think in terms of the goods economy, as though hardware (metal and plastic) were more valuable than software (intellect).

It is difficult enough to predict the future without being hobbled by statistical illusions and hoaxes about the recent past. The fact is that the rapid increase in US employment in the past decade has been accompanied by rising productivity and rising real compensation, income and net worth.

5. Getting better with age

Another source of excessive anxiety, at least for the United States, is concern about ageing. As John Creedy and Richard Disney (1989, p. 367) remarked, "it seems as if those demographers who have not been fully occupied in arguing that rapid population growth constitutes a major threat in one part of the world are warning that fertility decline constitutes a serious issue for the rest".

Like the declining share of employment in manufacturing, ageing is nothing new. The percentage of the US population over age 65 was 4 per cent in 1900 and 12.5 per cent in 1990, and is now projected to reach 12.7 per cent by 2005 (Hurd, 1990, p. 565). As mentioned earlier, and shown in Table 3, the 1992 census projections show much lower dependency ratios than were expected as recently as 1989.

Indeed, Americans of working age are now expected to account for a substantially larger share of the total population in 2010 than they did in 1990. That situation supposedly reverses itself between 2010 and 2030, but demographic projections beyond twenty years are quite hazardous – as the revisions between 1989 and 1992 demonstrate.

The dependency ratio is a demographic concept, not an economic one. It is true that a larger percentage of such "dependants" in the future will be older people rather than children. Unlike children, however, many people beyond the age of 65 are still quite capable of earning income, if tax and transfer policies do not encourage premature retirement. In addition, many will have substantial assets. It has been estimated that the baby boom generation will inherit as much as $10 trillion, in current dollars. And most baby boomers, unlike previous generations, will retire with assets of their own thanks to

Table 3. **Change in the US census estimate
of the dependency ratio between 1989 and 1992**

	1989 estimate	1992 estimate
1990	62	62
2000	63	61
2010	60	56
2020	67	62
2030	77	71
2040	78	70
2050	78	69

Source: Ahlburg, 1993.

the rapid proliferation of defined contribution plans, which typically involve employers matching employee savings which are then invested in a variety of mutual funds.

Some misunderstanding about ageing in America stems from confusing an increase in the proportion of older workers in the next two decades with a possible increase in the proportion of retired people in later decades. An IMF study, for example, says "an older population will consume more of aggregate disposable income [*i.e.* savings rates will fall]... and decrease the labour supply" (Masson and Tryon, 1990, p. 453). But a Dallas Fed study (Hill, 1989, p. 7) says, "as the population ages, national saving and net exports are certain to rise". The difference is that the IMF economists are assuming that retired people will constitute a rising percentage of the population, while the Dallas Fed economist is assuming older workers will constitute a larger portion of the population. For the United States, at least for the next two decades, the Dallas Fed conclusions are correct. In the absence of new tax disincentives, middle-aged baby boomers will save a larger fraction of higher incomes. Unless a substantial fraction of those savings are invested abroad, the US current account deficit (capital surplus) should soon vanish.

An ageing workforce is nothing to worry about. Older workers are relatively skilled and productive, earn higher incomes, pay higher taxes, save a larger fraction of their incomes (and do not invest as much in housing), and suffer much less frequent spells of unemployment. Switching from a younger to a middle-aged workforce should therefore raise productivity, further increase the proportion of families with relatively high incomes, raise real government revenue from all varieties of taxes, increase savings, and reduce average unemployment. The United States should welcome these sorts of problems.

The fact that relatively more workers will be in the years of peak earnings will increase the measured "inequality" of incomes, though not in a way that most people would consider unfair. Few people object to raises and promotions as they grow older. The later effect of having retired people make up a larger proportion of the population, beyond 2020, is less clear. There has been considerable variation in income and wealth among retired people, even when in-kind transfer payments (subsidised medical care) are valued at cost. Many of those who retire in the distant future are likely to have sizeable inheritances, reverse mortgages, and much larger pensions; they will also have many more years in which to draw down those assets. For the next two decades, though, the increase in the average age of the working population is far more significant than the increase in retirees (except in Japan and Europe).

Some have speculated that older people are more risk-averse and more reluctant to relocate between jobs or regions. Yet there has already been considerable ageing of the US population without any clear evidence of a drop in either risk-taking or labour mobility. Older people have accumulated more assets than the young, which means they must account for most of the boom in seemingly risky mutual funds, including those holding junk bonds and stocks in emerging markets. And the rapid exodus from states with steeply progressive income taxes, such as California and New Jersey, appears to have been concentrated among high-bracket families, which are usually headed by middle-aged people. Once the children have finished school, there may be less reason to stay in one place.

Table 4. **Percentage of population over the age of 65**

OECD area	1960	1990	2000	2020
North America	9.1	12.5	12.8	17.6
Pacific	6.1	11.6	15.2	22.4
Europe	10.7	14.4	15.7	19.7

Source: Golini, Righi and Bonifazi, 1991.

Although ageing is not so great a challenge as once thought in the United States, thanks to increased fertility and immigration, it is occurring at a much faster pace in Europe and Japan, as shown in Table 4 (which exaggerates ageing in North America, apparently due to the use of those dubious 1989 estimates).

Looking beyond the next decade or two, a growing population of retired people who live well beyond age 85 could present serious fiscal problems in the United States and elsewhere. Such risks, however, can be alleviated if individuals are encouraged to develop their own alternatives to taxpayer-financed pensions, medical care and nursing homes. The United States has gone a long way toward developing private pensions to ease the burden on social security. The United States has only begun to raise the retirement age to qualify for social security pensions and is, in effect, means-testing retirement benefits by taxing them above relatively modest income levels. There will be more such *de facto* cuts and limits on benefits, and therefore no sudden "crisis" for social security. Nursing care and catastrophic health care are potentially more costly problems, partly because the trend toward healthy lifestyles will eventually mean many more people reaching extremely old age, and therefore requiring many more years of costly care. There is a need in all the ageing societies for information, certification and tax breaks to encourage people to buy their own long-term care insurance (including home care as an alternative to nursing homes) and catastrophic insurance. As many of us live to be 100 or more, it will not be prudent to rely on the generosity of future taxpayers for nursing care or exceptional medical treatment. The growing "grey lobby" may press for such transfers from the young, but the fiscal impossibility of meeting those demands must ultimately prevail.

6. Unemployment in Europe: irrelevant solutions to obvious problems

In 1991, those unemployed for a year or more constituted only 6.3 per cent of US unemployed. In 1990, such long-term unemployment accounted for 37.3 per cent of the unemployed in France, 46.3 per cent in Germany and 71.1 per cent in Italy (*OECD In Figures,* 1993, pp. 12-13). Roughly a third of Europe's unemployed have been in that situation for more than two years (Flynn, 1993, p. 38). Extremely high and chronic unemployment of young people is also considered a more serious problem in Europe, particularly in countries with high minimum wages per month rather than per hour (which virtually precludes part-time or temporary work). And, of course, recent levels of unemployment are about 11 per cent throughout Europe (compared with 7 per cent or less in the United States, even in hard times), and appear to be ratcheting upwards over time. This situation represents a deplorable waste of the world's most valuable economic resource, human capital.

Some have taken false comfort from the fact that output per worker has increased, but this makes a fetish out of productivity statistics. If the purpose of an economy were to maximise productivity, that could be done by finding the most productive worker in the country and firing all the rest. If the goal were to maximise employment, that could be done by destroying all farm machinery.

The cause of Europe's high level and duration of unemployment is no mystery. There are insufficient incentives for employers to offer employment and insufficient incentives for employees to accept many of the jobs that are offered. There is a wide tax and regulatory wedge between what employers pay for workers and what employees receive, after income and payroll taxes. This must cause a reduction in the supply of labour at any given after-tax wage; therefore, firms have to offer higher gross pay in order to attract and retain workers. This shows up as a rise in real compensation that exceeds productivity gains, and therefore increases unit labour costs. Measured in national currencies (to avoid controversies over exchange rates), the increase in unit labour costs in manufacturing from 1982 to 1992 was 12.7 per cent in the United States, 31.4 per cent in France, 33 per cent in Germany, 33.5 per cent in the United Kingdom, 66.8 per cent in Italy, and 68.1 per cent in Sweden (*Monthly Labor Review,* November 1993, Table 49, p. 141). Without comparable increases in the prices businesses charge, which would mean high inflation (and therefore even higher wage demands), the more rapid increase in unit labour costs in Europe must squeeze profit margins and reduce employment.

In short, much of Europe has a carrot-and-stick problem. Those who do not work receive generous and lengthy subsidies from those who do, so that moving from the ranks of the subsidised unemployed to the taxed employed may yield little net gain in living standards. In many European countries, as the *OECD Observer* article quoted above points out, "additional work effort leads to little or no increase in net (after-tax) income because incremental gross earnings are largely, or even fully, offset by marginal income taxes and the reduction, or complete loss, of benefit payments" (*OECD Observer,* 1993). The article also notes that by taxing the use of labour, payroll taxes may reduce employment, particularly of unskilled, low-wage workers (this is particularly obvious in eastern Europe, where payroll taxes are often 39 per cent or more). Severance pay legislation is also particularly hard on outsiders trying to get in; if dismissal costs are too high, employers may become unduly cautious about hiring those with lower skills or experience.

These are man-made problems that can easily be fixed by reducing marginal income and payroll tax rates, minimum wage rates and the duration and/or replacement rate of unemployment benefits. Yet this clashes with well entrenched beliefs about the virtues of egalitarian tax policies and the welfare state. As a result, there has been a search for alternative ways to increase employment.

In the Commission of the European Communities' 1993 annual economic report, *European Economy,* there is a discussion (pp. 101-102) of the "employment threshold [which is] defined as the minimal rate of growth of real GDP that must be reached before total employment starts growing".[11] This seemingly innocuous concept practically takes GDP growth as "given" by forces beyond human control (labour supply and productivity). That leaves growth as the constant and employment as the variable – and *that,* in turn, leads to pernicious advice to retard productivity growth and shorten the working week.

"Labour supply [in the EC] may be expected to grow at an average of about 0.6 per cent per year from 1993 to 1996 and at 0.4 per cent in 1997 to 2000", writes *European Economy.* "In those conditions, a GDP rate of growth of 2.5 to 2.6 per cent per year would simply stabilize the unemployment rate at an unacceptably high level."

"Labour supply", the report says, "is determined by three basic factors, *over which economic policies have little influence*" [emphasis added]. These factors are growth of the working-age population, net migration, and participation rates. It is simply not true that net migration and participation rates cannot be affected by the relative generosity of transfer payments to those who do not work, compared with the taxation of those who do. Net migration (*e.g.* a "brain drain") affects the quantity and quality of the working-age population. This recalls the earlier discussion about how changes in relative tax rates between countries exporting and importing labour appear to have reduced the schooling of recent US immigrants (and perhaps raised the schooling of US emigrants). Moreover, the relative generosity of tax-financed pensions, compared with taxable earnings, can also shorten the effective "working age". Recent US proposals to subsidise 80 per cent of health care insurance costs for those over age 55, for example, would surely increase premature retirement.

In 1991, participation rates based on US concepts were 66 per cent in the United States, 63.6 per cent in the United Kingdom, 55.5 per cent in Germany, 55.2 per cent in France and 47.7 per cent in Italy (*Monthly Labor Review,* November 1993, Table 48, p. 140). If Continental Europe were nearly as successful as the United States and the United Kingdom are at drawing working-age people into the formal economy, but no more successful than it has been in creating employment opportunities, measured unemployment rates in Europe today would be above the levels seen in the Great Depression. However, that certainly does not mean that low participation rates are a good thing. Massive under-utilisation of labour in Europe means greatly reduced real output, and therefore reduced real income. Enticing even more people to drop out of the labour force by subsidising early retirement or through shorter hours would further aggravate such waste. Subsidising employment cannot work either, because the subsidies must ultimately be financed by taxing other jobs out of existence.

Do tax policies affect participation rates? Two sceptical scholars from the Brookings Institution, Bosworth and Burtless, looked at the impact of the two reductions of US marginal tax rates (with no reduction in average tax rates) that occurred in 1982-84 and again in 1987-89. They found that "men between the ages of 25 and 64 worked 5.2 per cent more hours than would have been the case on the basis of past trends... and that married women worked 8.8 per cent more".[12] Overall participation rates in the

United States rose from 63.8 per cent in 1980 to 66.4 per cent in 1990. The United States did not merely create millions of jobs in the eighties, it also created millions more eager workers. Previous "trends" toward early retirement, and toward declining male participation rates among Blacks and Hispanics, were arrested in the eighties. This is a major reason why BLS employment forecasts through 1985 proved to be far below actual performance.

European Economy goes on to warn that "productivity increases... may push the employment threshold to a higher level". That is, with growth assumed to be 2.5 to 2.6 per cent, and labour force growth likewise treated as "given", unemployment would be even higher. "On the other hand, *a larger share of services in GDP (given the way productivity is defined in these activities), further increases in part-time work and decreases in average working time would push it downward*" [emphasis added]. The clear implication is that productivity gains are undesirable, since they would supposedly raise unemployment, given the assumed 2.5 to 2.6 per cent path of GDP growth. A shift to shorter hours, and toward service activities that are "defined" as less productive, supposedly offers relief from unemployment. This is bad economics and suicidal advice.

Productivity increases would not simply raise the "employment threshold" (*i.e.* the unemployment rate for any "given" GDP growth), they would also raise GDP growth for any "given" increase in employment. And neither the supply of labour (participation rates and net migration) nor the demand for labour is "given" – they depend on unit labour costs on the demand side and work incentives on the supply side. A more rapid increase in the labour supply, if it was profitable to employ the additional workers, would also raise real GDP growth. Reducing average hours per week would not simply reduce the "employment threshold"; it would also reduce the level and growth of real GDP. A policy of deliberately wasting even more potential workers is no solution to unemployment, and it would unambiguously reduce future living standards in Europe.

There is nothing wrong with people voluntarily choosing to work shorter hours, thus taking more income in the form of tax-free leisure. However, it would be quite unwise for European governments to mandate shorter hours, or to encourage short hours and low participation rates artificially through steep marginal tax rates above some modest income threshold. Human capital is going to become increasingly scarce and valuable in the industrialised world, making it simply foolish to adopt policies to discourage employment.

Richard Freeman (1993, pp. 1-6) writes that "the experience of countries in the 1980s is consistent with two potential trade-offs. First, countries such as the United States that had a poor record in productivity and real wage growth had better experiences with employment. Except for Japan, no country managed to do well on both of these levels. Countries that maintained stable wage distributions had worse experiences with employment (again excluding Japan). This suggests a second possible trade-off – between income inequality and employment". This too is bad advice. As was demonstrated earlier, the United States did not have "a poor record" in productivity or real compensation during the 1982-89 period of rapidly expanding employment. Moreover, Japan's supposedly strong performance until recently is probably due to overestimating the productivity of the country's labour-intensive service sector.

There is no meaningful trade-off between productivity growth and employment growth; properly functioning economies can and do have both. Rising productivity makes workers more valuable, and hence more attractive to hire (unless, of course, wage demands and mandated labour costs rise even faster than productivity). As Figure 2 shows, employment in the European Community has grown most rapidly when productivity was growing rapidly, with the exception of periods in which compensation costs outran productivity. The particular element of compensation costs that has been most troublesome was not due to labour unions but to government policy – namely, soaring social security taxes and mandated labour costs such as severance pay.

What about Freeman's trade-off between inequality and employment? Once again, this paper has shown that the big drop in real incomes of the poorest tenth or fifth of the US population occurred from 1978 to 1980, not while the labour market was tightening after 1982. And much of the apparent increase in wage "inequality" consisted of inequality of hours – that is, increased employment opportunities for those who wished to work part-time (such as young mothers and students). There was also a large increase in the percentage of families who earned more than $50 000 a year, which troubled academics but not those who rose from the "middle class". Income figures collected from tax returns do show sharp increases of income among the top 1 per cent, but this was largely because lower marginal tax rates increased the proportion of compensation

Figure 2. **Labour productivity, compensation and employment: European Community**

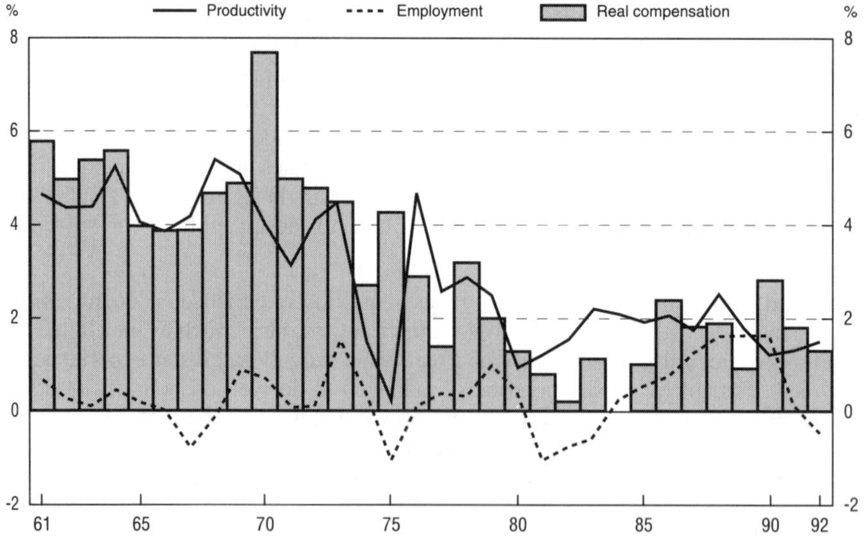

Source: Commission of the European Communities, 1993.

taken in cash, reduced the use of tax-exempt bonds and tax shelters, increased the realisation of capital gains, and reduced the incentive to under-report income.

There is, though, a sense in which a trade-off between inequality and employment does indeed exist. Tax and transfer policies that attempt to equalise after-tax incomes reduce the percentage of people who make the difficult efforts that are usually needed to earn high incomes. High marginal tax rates reduce investment in human capital, shorten the years of active work, reduce participation rates among spouses of high-income individuals, and reduce the willingness to take entrepreneurial or investment risks, to relocate, to assume more difficult work responsibilities, etc. Despite the renewed glorification of the "middle class" and berating of "the privileged", the harsh reality is that middle-income people rarely hire other middle-income people. Behind such flourishing young US enterprises as Microsoft and Wal-Mart were individuals who made a lot of money, and hired a lot of people in the process. If countries insist on using tax policy to punish increases in income above some modest level, they must also discourage the added output that would have created such incomes.

The egalitarian impulse is powerful in Europe, but it is nonetheless self-destructive and also futile. An OECD study (1985, p. 228) demonstrated that "the evidence for almost all countries suggests that the tax system overall has relatively minor effects on the income distribution". Overtaxed human or physical capital simply becomes more scarce, bidding-up the pre-tax returns to those who still have it.[13] Yet the whole economy nonetheless suffers from the artificial, tax-induced scarcity of exceptional efforts, talents and investments.

A National Bureau of Economic Research paper by Eric Engen and Jonathon Skinner (1992) reviewed nearly a dozen recent studies which found that increases in tax rates do lasting damage to economic growth. Engen and Skinner's own research, based on 107 countries over 15 years, estimates that "a 10 percentage point tax increase is predicted to reduce output growth by 3.2 percentage points per annum". Another study by William Easterly and Sergio Rebelo for the World Bank (1993, p. 32) looked at evidence going back to 1870, as well as recent comparisons between 28 countries. They too found "a negative association between growth and... the marginal income tax rate..." Yet another study by Philip Trostel (1993) found that even small increases in marginal tax rates have very large effects on young peoples' willingness to invest time and money in their education. A 1 per cent increase in tax rates was found to shrink permanently the stock of human capital by nearly 1 per cent; progressive tax rates had even stronger effects.

7.   Conclusion

The nature of employment is going to look much different by the turn of the century than it does today. In many industries, particularly knowledge-based services, commuting to work will be obsolete, as will fixed hours of work. Millions of people will work at home, communicating by computer with employers who will not necessarily be located in the same country, much less the same state. Smaller cities will attract more people, and mini-cities will spring up closer to where the people wish to live, rather than moving people to jobs. Such mini-cities will not simply be residential suburbs, but will include "industrial" parks (actually "service" parks), secure residential areas, and enclosed malls that offer food and entertainment as well as shopping.

Manufacturing firms will usually be smaller, as information technology erodes past advantages of vertical integration. They will also be more numerous, varied and competitive, with success dependent on the quality and speed of service, flexibility and niche products. Technicians will become far more important than operatives. There will be greater use of joint production with other countries, allowing countries that are relatively rich in technology and skill to outsource labour-intensive operations to countries with younger and expanding populations (such as Turkey and Mexico). Those Third World countries that offer secure property rights, sound money, free trade and reasonable tax rates will be able to tap world equity markets and develop at an unprecedented pace. Real wages will soar along with productivity in such "newly industrialised" countries, providing strong markets for the capital goods and business services of the post-industrial economies.

Service firms in the major economies will be larger, more capital-intensive, and dependent on a constant upgrading of technological capital and their workers' ability to use the latest software. All types of enterprises will economise on real estate costs by utilising space-saving technology and outside sources, particularly home labour. Organisation will become far less hierarchical, as will the division of labour.

There will be many more opportunities for self-employment, particularly among a wider category of "professions" – many of which do not yet exist. The most successful employees will be continually learning and thinking, regardless of the credentials they acquired in school. Schooling itself will become more innovative, more privatised and competitive, and less tied to classrooms. There will much less 9-to-5 routine work, and more flexibility of work hours. International labour mobility will increase.

In this environment, governments will have to take unusual care to preserve incentives for younger workers to invest in ugrading their knowledge continually, and to preserve incentives for older and secondary workers to continue working and acquire sufficient savings and insurance to meet the retirement needs of their families as well as the costs of their own eventual long-term care.

Mature professionals, managers and technicians in the stronger economies will commonly be capable of earning well over $100 000 a year in current dollars by 2005. Meanwhile, the costs of manufactured goods and food will command a dwindling share of household budgets, thanks to productivity gains as well as increasingly competitive production of labour-intensive goods from the Third World. The falling costs of goods will free up considerable disposable income to pay for better services, such as health care and education. It will also permit greater consumption of leisure, while still allowing a very comfortable standard of living. Motivating people to excel and to work up to their potential will become more difficult with new opportunities for the use of leisure, and the relative ease of meeting basic needs.

The increasing ability to reduce the number of hours per year devoted to formal employment, and to reduce the number of years worked per lifetime, will increase the sensitivity of the labour supply to marginal tax rates – particularly among workers with valuable knowledge and skills. Families that previously had two full-time workers will easily be able to take turns, with one spouse working full-time for a while and the other staying home or working part-time. The millions who will work at home as employees, contractors and consultants will easily be able to adjust the hours worked per year in order to keep their incomes out of high tax brackets. Greater flexibility of hours means people can be "partially retired" over a longer span of work years, achieving lifetime incomes equal to those they would have received had they subjected themselves to high tax rates on annual incomes above some threshold.

If the thresholds at which high tax rates apply are not increased as more and more families become capable of earning high incomes, or the rates reduced to competitive levels, other countries (and states) will use the lure of moderate taxation to attract human capital, just as some did with tax havens and tax holidays when physical capital seemed more important. It will be impossible to avoid such international tax competition by forming tax cartels (such as the minimum VAT in the EC), or by shifting from one sort of tax to another (because all taxes fall on those willing to supply human and physical capital to the formal economy). Countries that minimise marginal tax rates on human and physical capital will continue to prosper at the expense of those that do not.[14]

Governments can do little to create rewarding job opportunities. Even when they expand public employment, or subsidise private employment, the apparent increase in jobs must be financed by taxes, borrowing or printing money – all of which reduce employment and real earnings in the market economy. Efforts to "spread the work" by promoting short hours, early retirement or weak productivity growth must likewise fail, because they clearly reduce economic growth. However, governments can do much to minimise tax expenses and regulatory impediments that make it unattractive for investors to invest, for workers to work, and for employers to employ.

Notes

1. "By the next century, African-Americans, Hispanics and immigrants will comprise about 57 per cent of the new labour force, once dominated by white American-born males" (Pilenzo, 1990, pp. 49-50). This counts Black and Hispanic immigrants twice, and confuses the "new" labour force with who dominates the entire labour force.

2. Also, "the average science proficiency of 17-year olds in all racial/ethnic groups increased between 1982 and 1990" (US Department of Education, 1992, p. 48).

3. In the third quarter of 1993, unemployment rates among males aged 20 or older were 5.1 per cent for Whites, 11.3 per cent for Blacks, 8.2 per cent among those of Mexican origin, 12 per cent for Puerto Ricans, and 7.3 per cent for Cubans (who also have higher average incomes than Hispanics from Mexico or Puerto Rico). At the same time, 43 000 Hispanics claimed to be discouraged from seeking work because they "lacked education and training", compared with 33 000 Blacks and 124 000 Whites. Since there were over 3.9 million men and 13.7 million women who "do not intend to seek work", the fraction claiming that poor education or training prevents them from working was quite small (US Bureau of Labor Statistics, 1993, Tables A-56-59, pp. 59-62).

4. The authors suggested that "some corporatist nations, notably Sweden and Finland, have managed to restructure their economies successfully and the social compromise is likely to endure". Time has not been kind to this prediction.

5. Among Black women aged 25 to 34, for example, the ratio of median earnings among those with 16 or more years of school to those with twelve years of school soared from 1.24 in 1978 to 1.8 in 1990. Yet the number of new high school graduates (more of whom went on to college, and thus remained out of the labour market) fell from about 3.5 million a year in 1975-83 to fewer than 3.1 million since then (US Department of Education, 1992, Tables 31-2 and 66-1). As Kevin Murphy and Finis Welch point out (1993, p. 122), "the tremendous growth of the supply of more-educated labour with no corresponding reduction in relative wages is evidence that the demand for education increased greatly".

6. In the third quarter of 1993, there were 15.2 million voluntary part-time workers, compared with fewer than 3 million who were working part-time because "they could only find part-time work". Among those aged 16 to 24 and enrolled in school in September 1993, 4.9 million had part-time jobs, and 831 000 were seeking such jobs, while 1.2 million had full-time jobs and only 120 000 were seeking full-time jobs (US Bureau of Labor Statistics, 1993, Tables A-46 and A-7, pp. 51 and 15).

7. "The recent surge in overall wage inequality in Australia, Canada, West Germany and The United Kingdom appears comparable in magnitude to the sharp and well documented increase in the United States" (Davis, 1992).

8. "Of particular note were the significant increases of earnings inequality in the managerial and sales occupations for men and sales occupations for women" (Ryscavage and Henle, 1990, p. 14).

9. The first sentence of a recent Brooking Institution book says, "For nearly two decades the US economy has been plagued by... anemic productivity". Much later, the reader finally learns that "the slowdown in productivity growth began in the late 1960s... and was at its worst between 1973 and 1979" (Baily, Burtless and Litan, 1993, pp. 1 and 48). It is truly remarkable the way bad economic news between 1968 and 1980 is now routinely attributed to "the eighties", or to "two decades".

10. Note also this item from *The Wall Street Journal* (16 November 1993, p. A8): "Nikkeiren, a big-business lobbying group, says such Japanese industries as farming and services are only half as productive as America's. Catching up in productivity could mean Japan would have 5.8 million jobless people in the year 2003 – an unemployment rate of 8.6 per cent. Holding joblessness at current levels of 2 to 3 per cent would require such steps as job sharing and a big cut in working hours". This static, zero-sum reasoning from Japan is remarkably similar to ideas now circulating in western Europe, which are analysed in the last section of this paper.

11. It is noteworthy that the same report, when discussing Belgium (p. 41), correctly notes that "labour market disequilibrium reflects to a large extent the effect of high labour costs, including a large tax wedge, which discourages job creation". It also observes, on p. 130, that "the tax burden crucially affects the expected net returns on economic activity... governments face a sort of fiscal competition to which they will have to react by avoiding an excessive burden on those production factors which, through their mobility, can escape high taxation".

12. Cited in Joel B. Slemrod, "Progressive Taxes" in Henderson, David R. (ed.), *The Fortune Encyclopedia of Economics,* Warner Books, 1993, p. 341.

13. "Redistributive taxation...increases the attractiveness of lower paying occupations relative to higher paying occupations, and the resulting shift in relative labour supplies will increase the degree of inequality in the initial [pre-tax] distribution of income" (Wagner, 1989, p. 85).

14. This is a major theme of *Quicksilver Capital* by McKenzie and Lee (1991), particularly Chapter 6 – which graciously quotes this author as follows: "Countries, like companies, must compete in producing the most value at the lowest possible cost. Taxes are an important part of the cost of production, as well as the cost of living. Since people have to produce more in order to earn more, a tax system which penalizes added income will also penalize added output... Any country in which the marginal cost of government is not competitive will experience a loss of both real capital (a capital outflow) and human capital (a brain drain)".

Bibliography

AHLBURG, D.A. (1993), *Population and Development Review,* March.

BAILY, Martin Neal, BATOR, Francis, SOLOW, Robert *et al.* (1992), *Service Sector Productivity,* McKinsey Global Institute, Washington D.C., October.

BAILY, Martin Neal, BURTLESS, Gary and LITAN, Robert E. (1993), *Growth with Equity,* Brookings Institution.

BORJAS, George J. (1993*a*), "Immigration" in Henderson, David R. (ed.), *The Fortune Encyclopedia of Economics,* Warner Books.

BORJAS, George J. (1993*b*), "Immigration and Ethnicity", *NBER Reporter,* National Bureau of Economic Research, Fall.

BOUND, John and JOHNSON, George (1992), "Changes in the Structure of Wages in the 1980s: An Evaluation of Alternative Explanations", *American Economic Review,* June.

BUREAU OF THE CENSUS (1975), *Historical Statistics of the United States,* US Department of Commerce, Vol. 1.

BUREAU OF THE CENSUS (1993), *Statistical Abstract of the United States 1993,* US Department of Commerce, 113th edition.

BURTLESS, Gary *et al.* (1990), *A Future of Lousy Jobs?,* Brookings Institution.

CATTAN, Peter (1993), *Monthly Labor Review,* August.

COMMISSION OF THE EUROPEAN COMMUNITIES (1993), *European Economy: Annual Economic Report for 1993,* Brussels.

CREEDY, John and DISNEY, Richard (1989), "Can We Afford to Grow Older?", *European Economic Review 33.*

DANZIGER, Sheldon and GOTTSCHALK, Peter, eds. (1993), *Uneven Tides: Rising Inequality in America,* Russel Sage Foundation, New York.

DAVIS, Steven J. (1992), "Cross Country Patterns of Change in Relative Wages", NBER Working Paper No. 4085, National Bureau of Economic Research, June.

DOLLAR, David and WOLFF, Edward N. (1990), *Competitiveness, Convergence and International Specialization,* MIT Press, Cambridge, MA.

DRUCKER, Peter F. (1992), "Beyond the Blue Collar Worker", *Modern Office Technology,* December.

EASTERLY, William and REBELO, Sergio (1993), "Fiscal Policy and Economic Growth: An Empirical Investigation", paper presented to a World Bank conference, Washington D.C., 8-9 February.

ENGEN, Eric M. and SKINNER, Johnathon (1992), "Fiscal Policy and Economic Growth", NBER Working Paper No. 4223, National Bureau of Economic Research, December.

FLYNN, Padráig (1993), "Growth Is Not Enough", *International Economy,* November/December.

FREEMAN, Richard (1988), "Evaluating the European View that the United States Has No Unemployment Problem", *American Economic Review,* May.

FREEMAN, Richard (1993), "Working Under Different Rules", *NBER Reporter,* National Bureau of Economic Research, Summer.

GLYN, Andrew and ROWTHORN, Bob (1988), "Western European Unemployment: Corporatism and Structural Change", *American Economic Review,* May.

GOLINI, A., RIGHI, A. and BONIFAZI, C. (1991), "Population Vitality and Decline: The North-South Contrast", Report for the International Conference on Migration (Rome, 1991), OECD.

GRUBB, W. Norton and WILSON, Robert H. (1992), "Trends in Wage and Salary Inequality, 1967-88", *Monthly Labor Review,* June.

HILL, John K. (1989), "Demographics and the Trade Balance", Federal Reserve Bank of Dallas *Economic Review,* September.

HURD, Michael D. (1990), "Research on the Elderly: Economic Status, Retirement, Consumption and Saving", *Journal of Economic Literature,* June.

JOHNSTON, William R. and PACKER, Arnold H. (1987), *Workforce 2000,* Hudson Institute, Indianapolis.

JUSTER, F. Thomas and STAFFORD, Frank P. (1991), "The Allocation of Time: Empirical Findings, Behavioral Models, and Problems of Measurement", *Journal of Economic Literature,* June.

KIECHEL, Walter III (1993), "How We Will Work in the Year 2000", *Fortune,* 17 May.

KUTSCHER, Robert W. (1989), "Projections Summary and Emerging Issues", *Monthly Labor Review,* November.

LUCAS, Robert E. Jr. (1992), "Making A Miracle", *Econometrica,* Vol. 6.

MASSON, Paul R. and TRYON, Ralph W. (1990), "Macroeconomic Effects of Projected Population Aging in Industrial Countries", *IMF Staff Papers,* September.

McKENZIE, Richard B. (1988), *The American Job Machine,* Universe Books, New York.

McKENZIE, Richard and LEE, Dwight (1991), *Quicksilver Capital,* Free Press, New York.

MURPHY, Kevin and WELCH, Finis (1993), "Occupational Change and the Demand for Skill", *American Economic Review,* May.

OECD (1985), "The Role of the Public Sector", *OECD Economic Studies,* Spring.

OECD Observer (1993), "Growth and Employment", October/November.

PERLMAN, Lew (1992), *School's Out,* William Morrow, New York.

PILENZO, Ronald C. (1990), "Preparing for the Work Force of Tomorrow", *Modern Office Technology,* August.

QUINN, James Bryan (1992), *Intelligent Enterprise,* Free Press, New York.

REYNOLDS, Alan (1993), *The Impact of NAFTA on U.S. Jobs and Wages: A Critique of the Critics,* Fraser Institute/Hudson Institute.

RYSCAVAGE, Paul (1991), "Recent Data on Job Prospects of College-educated Youth", *Monthly Labor Review,* August.

RYSCAVAGE, Paul *et al.* (1992), *Studies in the Distribution of Income,* US Bureau of the Census, October.

RYSCAVAGE, Paul and HENLE, Peter (1990), "Earnings Inequality Accelerates in the 1980s", *Monthly Labor Review,* December.

SAUNDERS, Norman C. (1992), "BLS Employment Projections of 1990: An Evaluation", *Monthly Labor Review,* August.

SECCO, Samuel R. (1992), "Is Temporary Help An Economic Barometer?", *Office,* August.

SHELLY, Kristina J. (1992), "The Future of Jobs for College Graduates", *Monthly Labor Review,* July.

SILVESTRI, G.T. (1993), "Occupational Employment", *Monthly Labor Review,* November.

The Economist (1993), "Doleful", 9 December.

The Futurist (1993), "Too Many Graduates, Too Few Jobs", March/April.

TROSTEL, Philip A. (1993), "The Effects of Taxation on Human Capital", *Journal of Political Economy,* April.

US BUREAU OF LABOR STATISTICS (1992), *Employment and Earnings,* Washington D.C., November.

US BUREAU OF LABOR STATISTICS (1993), *Employment and Earnings,* Washington D.C., October.

US COUNCIL OF ECONOMIC ADVISERS (1993), *Economic Indicators,* Washington D.C., October.

US DEPARTMENT OF EDUCATION (1992), *The Condition of Education, 1992,* National Center for Education Statistics, Washington D.C.

US DEPARTMENT OF LABOR (1992), *Employment Cost Indexes and Levels, 1975-92,* Washington D.C., November.

WAGNER, Richard E. (1989), *To Promote the General Welfare,* Pacific Research Institute, San Francisco.

Value Changes and the Achieving Society: A Social-philosophical Perspective

by

Hans Lenk
Professor of Philosophy, University of Karlsruhe
Germany

1. Introduction

It is widely thought that unemployment, underemployment and other forms of involuntary inactivity will increase in the years ahead. Will this mean that in our traditionally work-oriented societies, where people define themselves largely through their work and jobs, men and women affected by these developments will lose their self-esteem and social status, and along with these a central feature of the meaning of their lives? It is the task of social philosophers to contemplate future trends in social and moral attitudes. This paper addresses from a social-philosophical perspective the topic of work values and examines some of the related social issues.

2. Changing values and attitudes toward work

Attitudes toward work, and working and living conditions, are undergoing important changes. Moreover, it now appears that gaps in attitudes among various segments of the population are widening in a process which can be loosely described as a "scissors effect" in societal development.

Over a number of years, the question "Is life more about work or more about pleasure?" was put to a representative sample of the German population by the public opinion institute Allens-bach. The results of the surveys (see Table 1), the most recent of which was conducted in 1990, show that – depending on the cohort – the perception of life as a task and a duty to society has diminished during the last four decades, whereas the perception of life as pleasure has increased considerably. The most interesting result is that the scissors effect shows up quite clearly between the under-30s on the one hand and sections of the older population on the other. In other words, a sort of generational cleavage in life-orientation has become remarkably prominent.

Table 1. **Life as work versus life as enjoyment**

Two people are conversing about life. The first says, "I consider my life to be a task which I am here to tackle and for which I have to mobilise all my resources. I want to accomplish something in my life, even if doing so frequently turns out to be hard and cumbersome".

The second says, "I want to enjoy my life. I do not want to struggle more than necessary. Indeed, one lives only once, and the main thing is to get something out of life".

	Share of total population (percentage)						
	1960	1964	1973	1977	1980	1982	1990
Life as work	60	59	48	48	51	43	62 (GDR) 18 (FRG)
Enjoying life	29	29	35	38	29	36	18 (GDR) 39 (FRG)

Source: Kistler and Strech, 1992; Noelle-Neumann and Strümpel, 1984.

An international comparative study on work ethics, also conducted by the Allensbach Institute, led to similar results. The question in the study was whether individuals engaged themselves fully in their profession, or whether they did just enough to satisfy the routine requirements of the job. In Germany, half of the population sample responded "I do my utmost, I put everything into my work" in 1967; in the 1980s, however, only 42 per cent considered this the summation of their personal attitude. In the United States, by contrast, the percentage of interviewees responding positively ("I do my utmost") over the same time frame remained at 68 per cent. Again, the age-group comparison was very revealing: older citizens in Germany still valued work very highly, whereas among the younger population an attitude of "enjoying life" prevailed – "You just do what you have to do and no more". This contrasts strongly with the United States, where the positive score for work attitudes is twice as high. Here, then, is an *international* scissors effect. (It should be borne in mind, though, that there may be methodological difficulties involved, such as those stemming from linguistic presentation.)

A cleavage also emerges in comparisons between different professional groupings. In particular, it seems that the higher the qualification, the greater the readiness to make a real personal effort to meet the requirements of the job, and the greater the identification with one's work. Among the highest-ranking white collar workers, civil servants and managers, almost two-thirds identify with their job to the extent of total commitment. With respect to the self-employed and the professional classes, the share is even higher, amounting to four-fifths. Among entrepreneurs and top-level managers in industry (EMNID study of 1984 – see Table 2), the trend is even more prominent: here, nine-tenths fully identify with their job. In other words, a kind of *status-oriented* scissors-effect is revealed. That top managers and the elite in every professional realm identify much more with their job than others appears to be as true today as it was in the mid-1980s. At the lower levels, however, there is a noticeable and increasing dissatisfac-

Table 2. **Work ethics**

(IFD Allensbach, 1982, percentages)

	Unqualified workers	Qualified workers	White collar workers (not in management)	White collar workers (in management)	Middle-management self-employed, professional classes	Entrepreneurs and top managers [1]
"I put everything into my job and often do more than is required of me. My job is so important that I would sacrifice everything for it."	28	35	34	61	80	90
"I do at work only what is required of me; no one can criticise me. But I do not see why I should toil beyond that. My job is not so important to me."	61	49	47	19	8	8

1. The percentages for entrepreneurs and top managers come from IWG (1984).
Source: Frankfurter Rundschau, No. 116, 21 May 1985, p. 10.

tion with the job: the workload is felt to be too heavy, and criticism in the presence of others is mentioned very often. There seems to be a feeling that the freedom of decision and control in the job has decreased.

More generally, this raises the question of whether there is a further, *attitudinal* cleavage, namely that between activism and passivity, and whether or not society is evolving into a new two-class stratification of enjoyers and performers.

Elisabeth Noelle-Neumann (1984) drew the conclusion that in the years to come, the identification with and pleasure derived from work would "decay", a phenomenon which would in turn generate a negative attitude towards the job and thus make proletarians of us all. She discerned a "poisoned atmosphere" at the workplace and "fatigue among its heroes", and attributed this to the influence of the media, critique-oriented education in school, and a tradition of authoritarian top-down management in industry. Her co-author Burkhard Strümpel, on the other hand, suggested that this might in fact be a positive adaptation of the workforce to a drastically altered work situation.

The views polled by the Allensbach Institute and by EMNID are put into perspective by data collected by Schmidtchen in the metal industry in the 1980s (see Table 3). Schmidtchen twice undertook a comprehensive study (1984, 1986) tracing indicators of work satisfaction (the results are broadly representative of other branches of industry). Workers who felt they were being employed in the right place mostly considered their work interesting and satisfying.

Schmidtchen developed a "resources" or "compensation" thesis to support his findings: the more means or opportunities of compensation a person has (the compensa-

Table 3. **Implications of different kinds of resources for job satisfaction: workers in the metal industry**

(percentages)

	Workload				Total
	High		Low		
	Resources				
	Few	Many	Few	Many	
Assessment of the job very good or good					78
Personal resources (competency)	15	79	52	94	
Organisational resources (competency)	26	66	78	91	
Financial resources (adequate pay)	36	59	81	94	

Source: Schmidtchen, 1986.

tion may have to do with degree of control, or be psychological, physical or financial), the greater the freedom of decision and action, and (therefore) the greater the satisfaction with the job. (This result is independent of whether the individual's views on technical progress are negative, positive or indifferent.) Those at the workplace who possess greater resources succeed better in coping with pressure and difficulties, *i.e.* with stress and strain.

Even for those workers who felt they had a heavy workload, personal resources such as competence, value orientation and education have a more significant influence on job satisfaction than organisational resources (whether one is supervisor or in a dependent position). Four-fifths (79 per cent) of those with a heavy workload considered their job and the assignment structure to be "very good or good" if they had substantial personal resources to compensate (compared to 59 and 66 per cent, respectively, with regard to financial and organisational resources). Values, commitment, and personal motivation, but also education and especially the scope for responsibility and independent action, are crucial in determining the degree of job satisfaction. Similar results were found with respect to the challenges posed by new technologies.

3.   The shift towards postmaterialism

One is tempted to ask whether the changes in attitude towards work really are as much a consequence of the change in values generally over the last decade as many authors tend to think. Has a fundamental, secular shift in underlying attitudes away from work and the values of achievement, acceptance and duty actually taken place? Conversely, is the reorientation towards enjoyment, self-fulfilment and self-development really that pronounced? To what extent are generational differences in attitudes simply a consequence of changed structural conditions?

The most interesting study with respect to this problem was conducted by Ronald Inglehart (1977). His own later overview of the topic, published in 1989, focuses on the situation in five EC countries and the United States (see Table 4).

Inglehart makes a distinction between two specific value orientations: the so-called materialist orientation towards meeting physical needs (of security, provision and care), and a postmaterialist attitude oriented more towards aesthetic, intellectual objectives and opinions, and values of solidarity (*e.g.* appreciating the beauty of cities and towns or nature, believing that "ideas count more than money", freedom of the press, the need for respect, affiliation and belonging). Thus, the values of self-development or self-fulfilment, both in the private sphere and (increasingly) in the professional realm, are confronted with the traditional values of acceptance and duty.

Inglehart tries to explain these vying orientations on the basis of two hypotheses. According to the first, the hypothesis of shortage, an individual's priorities mirror his or her socio-economic environment; one appreciates most highly those things that are relatively scarce. Physiological needs, fundamental security needs and so on – what Inglehart calls materialist tendencies – have priority standing in times of dearth, and lose their prominence in times of relative affluence and rising living standards. Conversely,

Table 4.   Value orientation – materialist v. postmaterialist – according to profession and age, European Community 1980-86
(percentages)

	Age								
	Under 35			35-49			50 and older		
	Mat.	Postmat.	N	Mat.	Postmat.	N	Mat.	Postmat.	N
Top management, civil service, public administration	19	27	(1 150)	23	25	(1 415)	24	15	(902)
Student	20	24	(11 677)	–	–	–	–	–	–
Self-employed	20	21	(869)	20	22	(608)	29	15	(505)
White collar worker	25	20	(11 623)	31	14	(7 166)	36	11	(3 871)
Unemployed	28	17	(4 958)	33	11	(1 218)	37	8	(1 565)
Independent businessman	31	12	(2 257)	40	9	(2 797)	41	7	(2 104)
Blue collar worker	30	13	(10 926)	36	9	(6 904)	41	8	(4 817)
Housewife	36	10	(7 787)	43	8	(7 192)	46	6	(9 824)
Farmer	38	11	(401)	45	8	(706)	46	6	(1 111)
Retired	–	–	–	37	11	(412)	46	6	(19 526)

Source: Inglehart, 1989.

the significance of differentiated social needs, particularly those of self-realisation and self-fulfilment, grows with the standard of living and the guaranteed fulfilment of basic physical needs. (Inglehart distinguishes these from urgent needs: clearly, hungry humans generally dispense with, or at least defer, the satisfaction of higher-level needs, given the choice.)

The second hypothesis is the so-called socialisation thesis: a considerable delay occurs in value adaptation since a person's fundamental values in mid-life reflect to a considerable degree those conditions prevailing during his or her childhood and youth.

Inglehart has conducted his empirical research since the 1970s in various societies, *e.g.* United States, western Germany (the Federal Republic of Germany before unification), the United Kingdom, Austria and the Netherlands. He concludes that in all these countries, in both absolute and relative terms, postmaterialist values are on the rise compared with materialist values such as economic and physical security. It is particularly clear that younger people are more postmaterialist than older citizens. According to Inglehart this constitutes not a short-term cyclical phenomenon but most probably an evolution away from the era of shortages and reconstruction following the Second World War. Particularly in the circles of younger technology managers, top managers, young professionals, politicians and students, postmaterialist attitudes have largely outstripped materialist values, a trend that seems to be representative of all the countries of the European Community. Only the self-employed, farmers and workers still represent traditional materialist values.

The postmaterialist trend seems set to continue (particularly in industrial working life), and will probably have a significant impact on such values as self-motivation (as opposed to compulsory work), education and career prolongation.

4. Leisure, technology, and the opportunities and risks for societal development

A combination of technological progress, keener international competition and (in some countries) high relative wages, together with a shift towards postmaterialist values, seems to point to a new balance between work and leisure time. How, though, is the transition to be managed?

Some philosophers (Byrne among them) recommend gradual adaptation, pacing the introduction of automation, retraining programmes, etc. Others, such as Adam Schaff, think that permanent education as a universal activity will solve the employment problem and at the same time lead to the realisation of the ancient ideal of man, *i.e.* universally educated, erudite and at the same time harmoniously developed (the Platonic *kalosk'agathós*). Clearly this ideal is utopian. In very few cases will a hybrid of *homo studiosus* (studying man) and *homo ludens* (playing man) replace *homo laborans* (working man). Few people wish to go to school their whole lives. However, as Albert Borgmann notes, this poses the question of the individual's capacity for making constructive use of free time. In his view, the quality of leisure activities is typically low, by any standard. Apprehensions that very little leisure time is spent on such activities as sports, the theatre, museums, performing music, correspondence or reading are borne out by social research. The total time devoted to these activities is, on average, only one-fifth of that spent watching television.

Borgmann concludes that the main promise of technology has not been fulfilled, either with respect to work or in terms of leisure; technology may have helped free us from the stress and tedium of daily life, but that feedom has been accompanied by an increasingly pronounced side-effect: a disengagement from reality. Our leisure contact with the world is being reduced to pure consumption, the uninhibited ''ingestion'' of commodities that require no preparation, provide no orientation, and leave no trace. That kind of diversion can only lead to distraction, fragmented attention spans and atrophied thought capacities. It is already apparent that people are not taking advantage of the new video technology's potential as a tool to help them develop into the historians, critics, musicians, sculptors, or athletes that they have always wanted to be.

Borgmann goes on to plead for reform ''on the leisure side of technology''. He proposes that the benefits of microelectronics and other advanced technologies be utilised to produce creative and recreative activities that engage us as full human beings, and engage us fully.

The microelectronic revolution may indeed be able to ''rid us of 'hazardous, dirty or monotonous work' '' – one could add alienating work to the list – ''and it can render the indispensable technological substructure of our lives more efficient and reliable''. Borgmann thinks that ''microelectronic devices can be helpful to these concerns, but they are not crucial''. However, it is far more likely that they are important and may even become crucial, though only as necessary but certainly not sufficient conditions of an active, full life. Interestingly enough, Borgmann stresses that ''those things and practices that... have orienting, engaging, and sustaining force are all of essentially pretechnological origin though they assume a new splendour and radiance when exercised in a technological context''.

What, then, can be said about the distancing effects of the modern technological world: the so-called ''administered'' world with its red tape, segmentation, functionalism, manipulation, etc.; the numbing effects of the highly codified world of film and television, the large and small screens that offer vicarious living, the illusion of an activity, pseudo-excitement without proper personal engagement? ''Telecracy'' and domination by the media generally is a real danger. Its power as a forceful, distracting, abstracting mediator between society members and ''reality'' should not be underestimated. Life itself seems not to be as genuine as the motion picture on TV. But ''Mediacracy'' is doomed – or at least conducive – to mediocrity. The near-homonyms often seem synonymous.

Indeed, an ideal, perfectly efficient new computer variant of the administered world seems to be on the horizon. It should be remembered, however, that abstract modelling by computers is just that – abstract. Models may seem to replace reality, shaping it to a hitherto unprecedented degree. Nevertheless, models are not reality. They constitute a mock-up world, one which might generate its own diseases. An advanced form of the ''computeritis'' described long ago by J. Weizenbaum seems to be generating a neurosis much like the one suffered by the book addict (*Bücherwurm*) of old. The public is well aware of the activities of hackers, both through fictional films such as *War Games* and actual news headlines. Computers apparently do exert a seductive force, which can lead to obsession and, in extreme cases, even illness. The point here is that leisure computer "activity" indeed distracts the user away from personal – *i.e.* person-to-person – involvement, and toward a new form of alienation.

5.   Achievement as a guiding value

Men and women, as active beings, need to cultivate creative activities in order to develop their personality. This can only be done by performing actions, with the aim of either creatively producing something or improving an existing level of performance. There is, in fact, a strong link between creative activity and recreative activities. Motivation in sports – as well as in the arts – has much in common with the motivation behind any creative activity. Creative, achieving activities generate opportunities to demonstrate excellence – even relative (*i.e.* personal) excellence – according to standards of individual talent and proficiency, and offer the possibility of personal involvement. This is important in a rather conformist society of institutions which nevertheless emphasizes individualism and individual values. Quite apart from the physical necessities, man needs meaningful tasks and goals. Any realm of creative activity could constitute such a goal. This is particularly true of the arts – performing arts included – and sports, exemplary realms of active personal achievement amenable to young people.

To be sure, a plea for the extended application of a principle of genuine, personal and authentic achievement should not be misinterpreted as an attempt to impose hard and fast rules on everyone and in all areas. That could eventually lead to an extreme dictatorship of achievement in the sense of Young's meritocracy. Ideas and guidelines cannot be pushed to utopian extremes. Adopting the achievement principle as the *only* social guideline would be as unjust and unfair as totally unfettered individualism in a free society. Extremes must be tempered by wisdom and reason, and by a sense of proportion and moderation. For example, one cannot and should not apply rigorous achievement standards to the ill, the weak or the old. Moreover, a universal, compulsory achievement principle would certainly contradict the above-mentioned idea of voluntary, authentic achievement. In fact, the shackles of a grim, all-pervasive and stubborn order would be counterproductive where really top-class achievement is at stake. On the other hand, if authentic achievement is engendered in a non-compulsory and open-minded educational setting, it can be attained more fully, with a high degree of enthusiasm and identification, even while standards are indeed met.

If developed and fostered in a moderate and humane form, the principle of personal or authentic achievement can have considerable educational significance – particularly in a society such as ours, which seems to rely so heavily on passive consumerism, prefabricated products, and administrations and institutions tending to override individual activity, in a world of media bombardment which encourages image-gluttony, complacent attitudes, and a tendency to take it all too easy.

It becomes increasingly obvious in a growing leisure society that man's longed-for paradise cannot be passive, hedonistic, or vicarious. Rather, it should be the opportunity for action, the chance to engage personally in communicative and co-operative activities in any creative realm that fosters an active life together with others.

6.   Creating a positive culture

One indispensible guideline in contemplating the future of work and society from a social-philosophical point of view is to develop and foster the idea of a socially just and comprehensive division and distribution of labour – in other words, to provide all people willing to work with at least a chance to obtain work. This could well imply reductions in overtime work, the shortening of working time and (in particular) the promotion of job-sharing.

It no longer seems sufficient merely to recommend life-long education, as the Polish philosopher Adam Schaff did in his report to the Club of Rome on the microelectronics revolution, *For Better or for Worse.* This is an interesting and important idea, but it will not in itself solve the problems of tomorrow's societies. The socio-philosophical case that has to be made is that it is essential to dispense with the stark traditional choice between work and starvation. In an industrial, affluent society, there should be a guaranteed minimum social standard of living (a basic rent or guarantee of sustenance) for everyone, whether they are working or not. The amount should, in line with the performance of the economic and societal system, considerably exceed the minimum necessary for survival. The social strategy of "satisficing", Nobel laureate Herbert A. Simon's term for guaranteeing basic sustenance, seems a wise and manageable one – at least in highly productive societies.

This does not mean, however, that the achievement principle should be totally ignored. Beyond the guaranteed level of sustenance, personal achievement and accomplishment could still be a socially differentiating and relatively "just" vehicle for distributing traditional or excess income and other social gratifications. At the same time, an affluent and welfare-oriented society should be able to dispense with the conventional link between work and survival. Such a change would offer new opportunities for voluntary activity, particularly unremunerated social work, and help to elevate such activity to a higher social standing.

Indeed, there is a whole raft of productive, socially worthwhile and creative activities outside the traditional assessment framework of job status and financial rewards. The postindustrial production system looks set to push affluent societies in that direction, shifting the emphasis from the traditional work ethic to those realms which permit free personal and social commitment, and enlarging the scope for a re-evaluation and reordering of the concept of achievement. Remunerated work and income from professional work are not all that render life meaningful. There are many other socially meaningful activities that engender a particularly satisfying, humane way of life, namely caring for the young, elderly and disabled, engaging in voluntary cultural activities, etc. If societies melt down the traditional link between work and sustenance – and the microelectronic revolution, together with other trends of the upcoming automated postindustrialisation age, could lead there – will the scope for free personal activity and social engagement grow, and become much more important? The question takes on a major dimension with regard to educational, creative and recreative activities, all of which would need to gain positive social recognition in proportion to their degree of creativity.

We are and will remain active beings. Now as in the future, some people will identify with their paid work to the extent of workaholism (recalling the joke, "I have now joined Workaholics Anonymous, but I just don't have the time to attend their meetings!"). Be that as it may, the overall pattern of social gratification and the ranking of prestige need to be reconsidered. With respect to non-paid activities, there is still a lot of ground to cover. We will be obliged to change, or to completely discard, some elements of the traditional Western work ethic. We may still, and should, uphold the right for active people (and even workaholics) to perform at top level as much as they like, but the old rigid notions of work and reward need to have a bit of their thunder removed. Voluntary and freely chosen activities pursued for their own sake and value, or for socially creative or recreational purposes, should acquire new social value and status.

The frontier between the realms of labour and leisure will, and should, be opened. A new positive culture offering freely chosen, personally engaging, unalienated activity, and (thus) the opportunity for authentic achievement and performance, has to be developed. (That opportunity might even be considered a human right.) Such a culture would render competition – *i.e.* for personal gratification and upward mobility – less weighty, without totally eliminating the idea of tempered competition as a vehicle for progress and development (though only in addition to the basic "satisficing" guarantees). Instead of being deadly serious, competition would become symbolic, a kind of sport and means of self-advancement.

Leisure activities would certainly play a major role in the overall pattern of this future society, in order to offer basic satisfying and "satisficing" opportunities for personal activity and involvement. Indeed, a new study on German youth found that now more than ever before, young people are writing diaries, playing an instrument, actively participating in sports and creating pieces of art.

Life must be active. People can only shape themselves, develop, and know themselves through personal action and achievement. One might even be tempted to modify Descartes' "Cogito, ergo sum", extending it to "Ago, ergo sum" – "I act, therefore I am". Only in so far as a person acts and achieves personally is he or she an individual personality. Thinking is one variant of this, but thinking is not enough. There is a poster that depicts a musing gorilla; it reads: "I think, therefore I am – confused".

The main objective of any educational programme should be to educate towards active personal involvement, personal and authentic achievement, and individual as well as original thinking. Self-engendered, creative and recreative activity with which the student can really identify, and which is in itself productive, should be the main goal. Primary self-motivation has to be ranked higher than secondary motivation instilled by others. Educational programmes, practices and institutions thus far do not adequately take into account the central difference between the two motivations, between creative activity and simply meeting routine standards, between genuine education and drill or manipulation, between active productivity and imitation. Drill and dressage merely perpetuate the technocratic tendencies of the administered, datafied and codified world of formal institutions and organisations.

How, though, can a positive culture of achievement be created? Clearly, the education system would play a crucial, long-term role. Several avenues would have to be pursued simultaneously. To begin with, since educational institutions cannot require or for that matter directly engender personal commitment, they would need to cultivate a number of options representing different degrees of involvement in socially, culturally and/or work-oriented activities. A spirit of individualistic competition would also have to be nurtured, but only as one vehicle, one medium among others. It would need to be supplemented by group-oriented forms of achievement and teamwork to take account of the shift in production and industrial organisation more generally towards group control, systems control and responsibility for complex human and capital resource configurations. Thus, the society of the future is likely to require individuals with a pronounced capacity not only for achievement, but also – and equally – for co-operation.

The young generation must not be discouraged. We must ensure that those who comprise the future of our society receive the necessary opportunities to deploy and employ their motivation for activity and achievement.

7. A summary of central theses

i) Authentic personal action and achievement are marks of individuality, indispensable parts of personal life, core characteristics.

ii) There is a creative principle of achievement. Authentic achievement is decisive for self-assessment. It confers meaning and genuine internal gratification.

iii) The formal achievement principle is certainly not outdated, meaningless or fruitless, as many a social critic thought. Creative achievement will have an important educational function if there is strong identification.

iv) Self-motivated achievement should be distinguished from secondary motivation. Only self-motivated activity is creative, productive or recreative.

v) It is imperative to foster and multiply the opportunities for personal activity and achievement in all realms of society.

vi) Any form of creative achievement and active involvement which is easily accessible for youngsters should be developed and acknowledged as being of great educational and social importance. This is true for all forms of creative activities.

vii) The plurality of "natural" experiences and forms of actions can and should find their expression in leisure-time programmes for children and adolescents.

viii) Opportunities for creative personal activities and achievements should be fostered more than they have been hitherto (particularly in European schools), but also outside the school curriculum. Schools have to avoid an exaggerated channelling of the official routine, of organised egalitarianism, formal adaptation and standardization, secondary motivation and formal control.

ix) Despite necessary specialisation, the aim is not to produce specialised narrow-minded "disciplinary idiots" (*Fachidioten*).

x) Competition is but one vehicle, one medium among others. Individualistic competition is necessary and important, but it is not everything. It has to be supplemented by group-oriented forms of achievement, by teamwork and co-operation.

xi) Educational institutions have to cultivate a plurality of options permitting very different degrees of involvement.

xii) High achievements should be assessed as a creative expression of the personality. Extraordinary achievements are never the result of drill and compulsion.

xiii) Authentic achievement is and remains an expression of individual freedom of action.

xiv) Creative self-development can only be based on personal action, works or achievements.

xv) Achievement is not a mere natural phenomemon, but at the same time a psychophysical, sociocultural and intellectual accomplishment.

xvi) We are in need of a new positive "culture" of achievement and a humanised creative achievement principle.

xvii) A positive culture of achievement is amenable to and in need of more just assessment of achievements.

xviii) Achievement is more important than competition.

Bibliography

In English

BORGMANN, A. (1986), "Philosophical Reflections on the Microelectronic Revolution" in Mitcham, C. and Huning, A. (eds.), *Philosophy and Technology. Vol. II: Information, Technology and Computers in Theory and Practice,* Dordrecht – Boston – Lancaster – Tokyo, pp. 189-203.

INGLEHART, R. (1977), *The Silent Revolution: Changing Values and Political Style Among Western Publics,* Princeton.

SCHAFF, A. and FRIEDRICHS, G. (1982), *For Better or for Worse.*

In German

INGLEHART, R. (1989), *Kultureller Umbruch,* Frankfurt a.M.

KISTLER, E. and STRECH, K.-D. (1992), "Die Sonne der Arbeit: Arbeitseinstellungen als Forschungsgegenstand im Transformationsprozess" in Jaufmann, D., Kistler, E., Meier, K. and Strech, K.-D. (eds.), *Empirische Sozialforschung im vereinten Deutschland,* Frankfurt a.M. – New York, pp. 155-189.

LENK, H. (1976), *Sozialphilosophie des Leistungshandelns,* Stuttgart.

LENK, H. (1982), *Zur Sozialphilosophie der Technik,* Frankfurt a.M.

LENK, H. (1983), *Eigenleistung,* Zurich – Osnabrück.

LENK, H. (1987a), "Verfall der Arbeitsethik? Umfrageergebnisse, Gründe, Interdependenzen zum Wertewandel" in Lenk, H. (ed.), *Zwischen Sozialpsychologie und Sozialphilosophie,* Frankfurt a.M., pp. 275-298.

LENK, H. (1987b), "Werte als Interpretationskonstrukte" in Lenk, H. (ed.), *Zwischen Sozialpsychologie und Sozialphilosophie,* Frankfurt a.M., pp. 227-237.

LENK, H. (1992), *Zwischen Wissenschaft und Ethik,* Frankfurt a.M.

LENK, H. (1994), *Macht und Machbarkeit der Technik,* Stuttgart.

LENK, H. and MARING, M., eds. (1992), *Wirtschaft und Ethik,* Stuttgart.

LENK, H. and ROPOHL, G., eds. (1994), *Technik und Ethik,* Stuttgart.

NOELLE-NEUMANN, E. (1979), *Werden wir alle Proletarier? Wertewandel in unserer Gesellschaft,* Zurich – Osnabrück.

NOELLE-NEUMANN, E. and STRÜMPEL, B. (1984), *Macht Arbeit krank? Macht Arbeit glücklich?,* Munich.

SCHAFF, A. and FRIEDRICHS, G. (1982), *Auf Gedeih und Verderb,* Vienna.

SCHMIDTCHEN, G. (1984), *Neue Technik: Neue Arbeitsmoral,* Cologne.

SCHMIDTCHEN, G. (1986), *Menschen im Wandel der Technik,* Cologne.

Prospects of Social Cohesion in OECD Countries

by

Christian Lutz
Managing Director,
Gottlieb Duttweiler Institute for Social and Economic Studies
Switzerland

1. Introduction

Is social cohesion in OECD Member countries a problem, and if so, why? Underlying this seemingly straightforward question are at least two categories of problems. First of all, there is clearly a deepening societal split between those who are able to cope with and take advantage of the changes in their environment, and those who are not – which (obviously) creates social cohesion problems. On the other hand, throughout society and even on a worldwide level, there is the rather puzzling coexistence of two opposing trends: one towards big, uniform structures and another towards increasing differentiation on all levels, from regional to individual, and even inside the individual mind. While many consider this a problem, there are in fact others who regard it as part of the solution.

It is useful, therefore, to describe the kind of phenomena that are involved before asking what might be done about them.

2. The main trends

In selecting the main developments to be considered here, the emphasis is on a long-term perspective and those changes which are likely to remain important during the next ten or twenty years.

A turbulent world

The world began to be "globalised" even before 1989. However, the collapse of the Soviet Empire was the final breakthrough towards globalisation, since the bipolar power structure that had shaped not only the industrial world but the Third World as well was suddenly transformed into a unipolar one. The globe was becoming the relevant strategic space and market for sales, resources and investors. The existing financial, information and communications networks were precursors of this development. One could even perceive the beginnings of a kind of world management, based on an informal network of top economic and political leaders developing a common understanding of global problems and rules. At the same time there was a further leap towards a kind of global culture, characterised by rules of human rights, market economy and democracy, and by the mass products of Western media and industry. It could be said that European culture, in its simplified American version, had finally conquered the world. The end of history?

Quite the contrary. Globalisation is only one aspect of several fundamental trends that have been greatly accelerated by the breakdown of the Soviet Empire. It has itself shifted attention to other conflicts which had been masked by the cold war: the widening gap between the rich minority and the poor majority of the world and increasing competition for the use of limited global resources have put the North-South conflict into a new perspective, thus creating new structures of conflict. With respect to OECD Member countries, the implications of importing these tensions will constitute one of the main problems of social cohesion.

In addition, globalisation accentuates what has been called the continuation of world war by economic means. With increasing accessibility to markets for buyers, vendors and investors, the competition between world regions and countries as industrial locations has become fiercer than ever. The ensuing restructuring at microeconomic level has been intensified by the fact that the worldwide homogenisation of production and marketing modes is extending the area of competition from the Western world to low-wage regions. As a consequence, an increasing number of jobs are shifting from high-wage regions to eastern Europe, South East Asia, the Far East and Latin America.

This tendency will gain momentum once managers of small and medium-sized companies begin to think in global dimensions. It will affect all the categories of labour of non-academic character. Currently the unskilled and semi-skilled workers are affected most, but qualifications in eastern Europe are already high in many sectors and they are rising quickly in a good number of developing countries. Thus, an increasing share of highly qualified jobs in OECD countries will be affected, as demonstrated by the example of software development in India. The consequences are unemployment, fear, loss of perspectives, protectionist tendencies and a weakening of the trade unions, which can lead to radicalisation in the defence of particular workers' interests in some industries, or to a search for innovations in social partnership, collective bargaining and the shaping of labour market rules (as can be seen in the case of Volkswagen, one which the CEO of ABB-Europe, Mr. Koerber, compared to the fall of the Berlin Wall).

Thus globalisation has a profound, lasting and increasing impact on social cohesion in OECD countries. It will remain one of the main reasons for growing structural unemployment and subsequent social disruptions. At the same time, it will increase the pressure for social and technical innovation.

Paradoxically, globalisation is also strengthening regionalisation. In releasing the chains that locked countries and regions into the discipline of their respective Eastern or Western camps, it took away the blanket that had covered so many national and regional feelings and aspirations of identity. Whether regionalisation is breaking up existing national structures or reviving past ones is mostly a question of definition and specific historical background, as illustrated by the former Czechoslovakia and Yugoslavia, the Baltic states, the former members of the Soviet Union – and the civil wars raging in some of these countries.

Regionalisation, developing in parallel with globalisation, is also strongly felt in OECD Member countries. Today, the Europe of regions is already vital, multifaceted and increasingly calling into question traditional national borders. It is probably safe to say that the European Union will never become a federal state in the traditional sense, but rather a complex, dynamic network of national, regional and local bodies developing a multitude of pragmatically selective horizontal and vertical relations. Is regionalisation, as a whole, endangering social cohesion? Answering this question requires a closer look at its different aspects:

1. Regionalisation worldwide is creating a growing number of potential conflicts. At the same time, weapons of all kinds (with new forms ranging from computer network disruption to plutonium) become more and more easily and cheaply available and efficient. In addition, globalisation increases the efficiency not only of global corporations but also of Mafia networks and groups motivated by cultural and/or social frustrations to keep conflicts going. Thus our world, while having overcome the immediate danger of blowing itself up in a nuclear war, has become a much more dangerous place at the regional level.

   This is creating a threat to social cohesion in OECD countries, since worldwide regional struggles and their consequences are imported into OECD countries, as are the victims of economic disparities: immigrants from troubled regions, often from far-away cultures, and sometimes extremists, organised criminals, drug dealers, terrorists and simply people without any real subsistence or work qualifications. In an environment already characterised by fear of social decline, jealousy and budgetary restrictions limiting the capacity of social networks, this can easily lead to xenophobia, political radicalisation, social unrest and criminalisation of the poor.

2. However, there is a bright side to the picture. Increasing knowledge about other cultures and the problems of other groups, as well as changes in organisational behaviour to be described later, contributes to lowering thresholds and increasing the capacity for intercultural dialogue within OECD countries – i.e. between different regions and social groups – and on a global level, where such dialogue is becoming a necessary and extremely helpful approach to solving political and economic problems. In this perspective, regionalisation may indeed be a threat to social cohesion, but at the same time it shows how the problem might be overcome.

3. In western Europe and the United States, regionalisation has not been unleashed by the end of Soviet totalitarianism and is only partially associated with worldwide turbulence. In fact, it is the obvious answer to a number of necessities and desires, and is greatly facilitated by a number of new possibilities.

With respect to the necessities, the transport- and energy-intensive pattern of global and continental division of labour may not be sustainable in the long run or even economical in the short run, if the real costs to society are taken into account. Thus there will be a shift to more regional and local circuits, eventually supported by drastically rising energy and transport costs. At the same time, the increasing complexity of problems and the speed of change will entail shifting decision levels as far down as possible, in both politics and the corporation. Growing pressures towards flexibility in the labour market are also better handled in regional and local frameworks.

As for desires, increasing complexity and the speed of change in our perceived reality, rising consciousness of ecological problems and the change from purely quantitative notions of economic success to more quality orientations have shifted individual priorities: more people prefer conditions where work and private lives are closely linked in a social network of personal contacts, one close to their cultural roots, in surroundings they can influence, with good quality air, water, landscape and housing.

With the ubiquity of interactive computer networks, the advent of multimedia units replacing the car as the key technology shaping structures and habits, and the new organisational network pattern of small, decentralised, loosely coupled, autonomous units, people will have the possibility to organise themselves according to their needs and desires.

The coming years will almost certainly see the creation of what may be called the "new polis", small, relatively autonomous communities managed in a democratic way by their citizens, developing spontaneously rather than through central planning. This may prove the ultimate answer to problems of social cohesion: small communities as locations of small organisations working within international networks and offering jobs very much tailor-made to people living in the neighbourhood and developing, for their part, tailor-made networks of citizenship and social responsibility.

The flood of options

In most OECD countries, the average citizen has experienced an explosion of options during his or her lifetime. Since the Second World War, purchasing power has steadily increased – as has leisure time, especially as a percentage of lifetime; levels of education, professional qualifications and general information; and the choice of goods and services, professional activities, holidays, papers, TV programmes, films and other entertainment, etc. Moreover, the generalised acceptance of prescriptions for behaviour issued by conventions, churches, teachers, etc. has collapsed under the multitude of possibilities at hand.

The speed of change has exploded as well. The very fact that we assimilate a continuously growing number of units of information per unit of time is perceived as accelerating change in external reality. In addition, the exponential increase in our knowledge base is accelerating the obsolesence of existing knowledge. Both factors, together with the growing intensity of worldwide competition, progressively raise the pressure to adapt our structures and behaviour to quickening change, which in turn further quickens the change to which societies have to adapt.

Moreover, growing complexity and the higher speed of change increase synchronisation problems in society and organisations, thus reducing our degrees of freedom in time and hence the number of options that can be selected.

Of course, information and communication technologies (IT) help in coping with these problems – but only after having largely created them, since the explosion of options, particularly over the last quarter-century, has been due essentially to the effects of IT on labour productivity and on media production. Additionally, in helping people do more in less time, and thereby inspiring them to put a premium on time, IT is further accelerating change and further extending the dictatorship societies have accorded their time management systems.

Thus there can hardly be any doubt that the technical and economic development of this last half-century, which was thought to open an avenue towards human emancipation by creating a greater degree of individual freedom in shaping one's own life, has created a problem: the flood of options has turned into an increasing compulsion to select.

But is this problem endangering social cohesion in OECD countries, and if so, how? The answer may be found in looking at the selection strategies society employs:

1. There is a pattern identified notably in fundamentalists. Their point of departure is an absolute, fixed image of reality and set of values which serve as their perception filter. These are not amenable to examination, since they are self-evident and beyond doubt. Elements that do not fit are either warded off or attributed to the "evil" world of the enemy. On the basis of this definition, fundamentalism is not confined to religious and fascist connotations, but includes many petty bourgeois, technocrats, and political believers of various leanings who may have developed their own fundamentalist selection strategies. A broad assessment of opinion polls and cluster analyses suggests that in most OECD countries, as many as 20-30 per cent of the population fit this pattern. The strategy is very efficient as a means of orientation and of attaining short-term security in a turbulent environment. However, it also creates increasing problems for the fundamentalists themselves and the surrounding society.

   Since the inflow of information is continuously rising and changing, the shielding effort must also be stepped up, thus cutting the fundamentalist off from a growing number of potential realities which may be relevant. As a consequence, fundamentalist groups not only become (by necessity) increasingly radicalised and less and less capable of communicating with their social environment, but they also fail to develop the qualifications needed to cope with changing life conditions. This attitude is a danger to social cohesion, not only because it leads to escalating conflicts with the outside world – including other fundamentalist groups – but also because the inability to cope produces unemployment, poverty, family and health problems. Fundamentalists are easily manipulated and seduced by demagogues, gurus, criminal leaders, drug dealers, etc. Once their shield becomes ineffective and they discover they have been misled, the resultant instability and frustration may create additional social tensions and problems.

2. A totally different selection strategy is that of individualism. Individualists try to develop their model of reality, behaviour, values and priorities according to their experience, in a lifelong dialogue with the outside world as they perceive it. In Niklas Luhmann's sense of "meaning of life" or "meaningfulness", they are "meaning-orientated" (*sinnorientiert*): their criterion in selecting from several options is what corresponds best to their self-description. Individualism, according to this definition, is highly efficient as a selection strategy that is well adapted to the person and his or her environment in the short run; in using incoming information to develop further the image of reality and the notions of reasonable behaviour, values and priorities, it is also sufficiently flexible to cope with a changing world.

Is individualism, then, not a problem for social cohesion? Many conservative observers think it is; they are convinced that a society without generally valid and accepted values and rules will fragment and cease to exist. Furthermore, they believe that society needs some kind of authority in order to preserve and disseminate this set of values and rules.

While it is certainly very useful to have a generally accepted set of values and rules as well as the appropriate institutions to uphold and diffuse them – such as, for instance, a legal system – it can be fatal to a society or an organisation to lose the capacity to adapt to a changing environment. Yet if a society were to try to adapt itself to an increasingly complex and quickly changing environment largely by means of centrally determined rules, it would soon suffocate from its *own* complexity. Thus, in order to be capable of acting while being well adapted to a complex environment, it is essential to define only what has to be defined, and to do this at as low a level as possible.

In individualism, while each person remains well adapted to his or her quickly changing environment and is hence able to cope with it, this does not imply any lack of co-ordination. Individuals developing in similar surroundings will develop similar images of reality and sets of rules. In the course of cultural history, societies have developed languages and other conventions that help them if not to understand each other, then at least to arrive at relatively efficient hypotheses about what the others might have meant. In the course of biological evolution, humankind has developed some common ground of understanding, organs of perception and instinct with their triggering mechanisms. Thus, there may not be a need for additional central authorities imposing rules apart from those generally accepted by the individuals concerned. An individualist society may develop a highly flexible set of rules, differentiated in the sense that at the most general level there may be agreement on rules like tolerance, empathy etc., while a family or a corporate division might wish to be much more specific; and it will keep the process open in the sense that any set of rules can be developed further in the dialogue between those concerned. In this sense, as with regionalisation, individualisation does not produce a problem of cohesion; rather, it offers the solution in that it produces the necessary degree of cohesion without endangering the basic level of differentiation and flexibility required in a complex and dynamic environment.

3. There is a third selection strategy, the behaviour of "connected multiminds". At first one may doubt whether this should be considered a selection strategy at all, since it looks like a mixture of indifference and arbitrariness on the one hand, and compression of complex events, lifestyles and scenarios into bits and bytes of the shortest duration on the other. Putting a whole biography into one videoclip, zapping from one world to another in seconds, watching several movies at the same time, jumping from Wall Street to Baghwan without the slightest hesitation – everything seems to be of equal validity and equal value (in German, *gleich-gültig, gleich-wertig*) in its own context. This attitude seems to prevail among those of the younger generation who do not belong to the frustrated class that tends towards fundamentalism.

It is tempting to say that the difficulty in finding an orientation in the midst of the flood of options can be overcome simply by abandoning the idea of orientation and letting oneself drift with the flood. However, this is looking at a new attitude from the perspective of traditional individualism, which itself asks for a clear and coherent set of values and rules. In fact, this perspective is determined by an image of man which begins to evaporate in the psychology of multimind (Robert Ornstein, Kenneth J. Gergen). The Freudian notion of an ego more or less rationally controlling the hierarchy of needs and the exchange with one's environment, possibly supervised by a superrational "self" (according to Jung), is replaced by a dynamic network of minds with their own triggers, modes of functioning, values and images of reality. No one mind dominates the game; during the interactions of different minds with each other and with the outside world, the focus of attention moves from one mind to another.

Obviously, this image of the mind resembles a pattern already encountered in relation to future organisations: the self-developing network of interrelations between small autonomous units. Therefore, multiminds are particularly well adapted to a complex, rapid-change environment. It could also be said that they have overcome the limitations traditional individualism imposed on the use of brain potential by suppressing, as far as possible, any notion that was incompatible with traditional rationality. Thus, they dispose of much larger perception filters and provide much quicker, more immediate modes of information processing without overloading the system, because they concentrate on a limited sector of reality at any given moment, and develop extremely high speeds in adapting to fluctuations in the environment.

With respect to social cohesion, the same principle that applied to individualists applies here: connected multiminds are a tremendous problem in the eyes of those who believe that in order to maintain cohesion, there must be a well-defined, generally accepted set of values and rules. If society is considered as a self-organising network of interrelations among largely autonomous units, multiminds are not a problem, but a solution.

4. Of course, the categories mentioned so far are largely simplified mental models which, in this pure form, are hardly to be found in real society. It is impossible to know the percentage of individualists and multiminds in OECD countries, since polls do not ask the question, and cluster analyses show precisely that: clusters of behaviour or attitudes. A fair estimate would be that about 10 to 20 per cent of the urban population of Europe and North America roughly correspond to one of these two models, and that individualists are more frequent among those over 40, while multiminds are predominantly represented among those under 30. The rest are just emulators, fluctuating somewhere between several paths of self-development. It may be said that the biggest danger with regard to social cohesion is that in their fluctuations they may feel that they are losing their orientation or that they are failing to cope with professional requirements, and consequently drift towards fundamentalism.

Demographic trends and the future of the family

The two fundamental demographic trends in OECD Member countries are well known: generally shrinking populations – birth rates far below the stabilization level of 2.1 – and a rapidly rising percentage of older people, partly a consequence of low birth rates and partly due to a standard of living that enables more people to grow old. A third will probably play an increasingly significant role in the future: immigration, especially from nonmember countries, which even now is partially offsetting the two indigenous trends.

Demographic trends are both cause and consequence of societal and economic changes, and they have an important bearing on social cohesion.

First of all, with regard to births, industrialising countries usually go through a fundamental change from a "wasteful" to a "thrifty" population mode (Mackenroth), *i.e.* from a combination of high birth rates and high mortality to one of low birth rates and low mortality. Apart from the medical innovation factor, this is essentially due to the fact that children, economically speaking, turn from an asset into a liability. Consequently, they compete with "other" goods and services that limited purchasing power can provide. In addition to accentuating this competition, the flood of options has induced a growing number of women to join the workforce in order to enlarge their purchasing power and take advantage of the increasing opportunities of professional and, hence, personal fulfilment offered by modern civilisation. This is an additional dimension of the competition between births and other opportunities: it produces a fundamental conflict between raising children and other activities in the female biography.

There are many striking examples of this type of interaction:

- the breakdown of birth rates in Catholic countries such as Italy and, even more so later on, Spain, once the practical emancipation of women had been set in motion by an increasing labour demand due to dynamic economic development;
- the truly dramatic "birth strike" in eastern Germany that set in after 1990, once public services that had dealt quite efficiently with the conflict between nursing

needs and mothers' professional activities were abandoned, and professional perspectives became increasingly sombre;
- the Swedish case: the years since 1980 have seen clearly rising birth rates, apparently because women feel that social systems are coping sufficiently with the conflict between children and profession.

At this point, it is already possible to identify one problem that demographic trends pose for social cohesion. The fact that ever fewer active people have to support more and more retired persons produces an increasing strain on social systems and, hence, on solidarity between age groups. Moreover, that phenomenon is only one of several factors; the unemployed, an increasing share of immigrants, and other groups are adding to a rising share of the population being supported by a shrinking minority.

It is useful to recall why solidarity between the professionally active minority and the rest of the population has become a problem of such importance. Before the Industrial Revolution, the three-generation family had been the centre of subsistence in almost every respect. Afterwards, it gradually lost this function and virtually vanished – a development accelerated by the greater mobility of the young and, recently, even of older people. We leave our homes for the sake of professional opportunities and, as senior citizens, for pleasanter surroundings. Immigration is another dimension of mobility. Both kinds tend to disrupt the small family and neighbourhood networks of mutual solidarity, and hence increase the demands for anonymous public systems to replace them. Once these systems (unsatisfactory as they may be) break down under stress, there is nothing left. In addition, the motivation to prevent the systems from breaking down is fading away, because the burden of the shrinking minority that supports them is growing, and because increasingly that minority fails to understand why it should support people it hardly knows, many of them coming from other continents in order to participate in the country's wealth.

It is clear that the process of social erosion (*i.e.* of traditional family ties) did not stop with the three-generation family. Today, even the "classic" two-generation family consisting of the parents and their one-to-three children is out. To take the example of Switzerland, already in 1980 singles represented 29 per cent of all households; another 30 per cent were two-person households, many of which were single mothers living with their child; 35 per cent of the Swiss population lived in one- or two-person households, and in urban agglomerations the percentage was much higher. If the time dimension is added – less and less people living together are married, and of the marriages one-third will end in divorce, the majority of these at the request of the women – then clearly it is no exaggeration to speak of an erosion of the family.

Behind that erosion lies a process of mutual reinforcement with individualisation. On the one hand, the flood of options and the evaporation of fixed rules and life models are removing the pressure towards marriage and staying together just by moral obligation. On the other hand, the children that have been raised by their mother – or, in some cases, their father – alone or living with several partners, possibly with brothers and sisters from different parents, removed from the wider family of aunts, uncles and cousins, are heavily programmed towards individualism and against any stereotypes of family or of male and female roles. They are often on their own and have to become "autonomous" earlier, which may help to develop adult patterns but may also create additional orientation troubles. At the same time, the matrimonial line is becoming more important, as are "female patterns" in attitudes, behaviour and values.

What are the problems that the erosion of traditional families creates for social cohesion? The strain on the system caused by the changing age structure has already been mentioned. Additional stress is produced by the risk single parents face of slipping into the class of the new poor. Even well educated mothers tend to be the first to be fired once the number of jobs is reduced, because they are not – or are thought not to be – able to invest all their energy in their jobs. In addition, the percentage of single mothers with less-than-average professional experience is particularly high due to the unsolved conflict between child-raising and professional activities. Thus, unemployment is particularly high in this group.

In addition, the number of households and of square metres per inhabitant has constantly risen during the past decades, due to the proliferation of single and two-person households and the increase in purchasing power. Especially in urban agglomerations, this places a continuous strain on the housing supply and causes apartment prices to skyrocket, even in low-price neighbourhoods. This is affecting precisely those young mothers – and parents – who have to move to urban centres in order to earn their living. It is only one of several examples explaining why especially in the case of young urban mothers and parents, the income threshold that represents poverty is high and still rising, and shows hardly any downward flexibility. Thus the danger of sliding into poverty is becoming more widespread.

This kind of problem will also become more widespread over the generations since children of poor households will, on average, receive less education, live in less prosperous neighbourhoods and sometimes get involved in networks of crime, drugs and prostitution. Later on, they will tend to be unemployed because they lack qualifications, and disoriented because they lack education. They risk becoming "atoms" in the lonely crowd who are particularly vulnerable to all kinds of fundamentalism.

Here again, however, the picture is not completely bleak. The new poor will remain a minority. It is already clear that the average level of education and professional skill of women is rising. At the same time, the trend towards more flexible labour arrangements has been accelerated by the recent recession, and will be supported further by future organisation patterns, invidualisation of lifestyles and the increasing weight of female attitudes in organisations and private life. In addition, the trends mentioned earlier that point toward the "new polis" will produce a wave of "tele-working", partly at home and partly in offices and factories close to home.

In this context it is evident that the erosion of the traditional family is not necessarily leading to a fragmenting of society. On the contrary, it is caused by and is leading to an individualisation of family life in general. There will be more ways of living together – several parents sharing the education of their children, working partly at home, partly part-time outside and partly not at all, developing some small enterprise together, co-operating in a neighbourhood network, developing new social services, etc. In the framework of a tailor-made constellation of family, neighbourhood, friendship, professional and public networks, services and systems, an increasing number of women will find the combination suiting their capacities and desires; as the Swedish example seems to indicate, this could even stabilize population trends.

Thus, at the family level, it is (again) not individualisation as such that is the problem; individualisation could in fact prove to be part of the solution in the long run. The danger, once more, is the widening gap between a majority which is able to cope, and an increasing minority which is not.

This leads us to a final word concerning immigrants, and especially those who left their countries to escape political pressure or absolute poverty, since the others, such as professionals migrating within the OECD region, do not, in general, pose a particular problem. It is obvious that the deprived immigrants add to the problems mentioned so far. Their cultural and professional background often does not provide them with the kind of education and skills they would need to orientate themselves in this new, complex and turbulent environment and find a job, let alone develop a professional career. In addition, they are usually either kept in ghettos without many opportunities to get acquainted with their new environment, or established in neighbourhoods dominated by the new poor, the unemployed, the disoriented, the lower-class fundamentalists – *i.e.* by those who regard them as competitors and enemies, who are open to racist and xenophobic tendencies and without the kind of communicative competence necessary to engage in an intercultural dialogue of mutual learning. Moreover, very often the immigrants have already delivered themselves into the hands of organised crime in order to reach their country of destination. As a consequence of ongoing cultural, human and economic deprivation, they become easy victims of further criminal activity. There is reason to believe that this trend, with its clear potential for disrupting social cohesion, is only just beginning.

The twilight of the dinosaurs

As was pointed out earlier, the collapse of the Soviet Empire was only the most obvious failure of an organisational pattern that the West too had followed, namely of huge, centrally planned, hierarchical mechanisms in public administrations, armies, churches and private companies. Until recently, in fact, the internal workings of companies bore no resemblence whatsoever to the "invisible hand" of the market economy. This fact was not surprising since it was an immediate consequence of the scientific paradigm, *i.e.* the concept of reality that had prevailed during several centuries of industrialisation: a Newtonian world controlled by an independent and hence sovereign Cartesian mind. As in science, this paradigm has been extremely successful as an organisational model in the Western economy. And, as with every successful paradigm, it has transcended its own limits and become the victim of its own success. There are several dimensions to this in the present economic situation:

a) Huge mechanistic systems produce their own, partial rationality: the economy has tended to "externalise" the costs these systems impose on their environment and on future generations. Such externalities are not only ecological. The mechanistic pattern also tends to repress the fact that the human beings who depend on it are not "sovereign" but, as Karl Marx put it, "alienated". Since the very success of these organisation machines created a flood of options and, hence, increasingly independent individualists, they produced a type of worker, consumer and citizen to whom the pattern was no longer acceptable. Legitimation became a problem.

The same is true in politics: its partial rationality tends to externalise those problems to which political institutions, especially highly structured government organisations, are ill-adapted. This is particularly the case with long-term problems that override the competences of specific services. Since – as was demonstrated by Mancur Olson in *The Rise and Decline of Nations* – there is a law of increasing specialisation in politics and public administration, real problems are increasingly ignored by the political structures, thus creating a problem of legitimation, of ungovernability and of anarchy.

Externalisation of environmental costs and of problems to which political structures are ill-adapted affects the fundamental consensus necessary to preserve the "societal contract" (*contrat social*); in addition, the mounting burden of unsolved problems is a source of growing structural budgetary troubles and social problems – the resolution of which may increasingly involve recourse to criminal organisations and even terrorism. Furthermore, the scope for dealing with social conflicts merely by distributing growth is shrinking, leaving every group to a fierce defence of its vested interests.

b) A second dimension is that our highly structured organisation machines, by virtue of their success, created the increasingly complex environment described above. Since, in order to keep in contact with its environment, an organisation must develop the same degree of complexity, a complexity race emerged which was inevitably lost most dramatically by the least efficient organisation, namely the Soviet Empire. The centrally planned economies of the West, the big corporations, were helped by information technology, and by the external market; however, in the end, they grew either too complex to maintain their capacity to decide and act, or they lost touch with their environment – or, mostly, both. Since this coincided with pratically all the other problems mentioned in this paper, many of these big corporations had to lay off tens of thousands of employees, and this process is far from reaching its end. At the same time, however, an appropriate counter-trend developed from these difficulties, namely a new organisational pattern, of which ABB is an example. This will be treated in more detail in Section 3.

c) Mechanistic organisations call for precisely defined functions and parts and, hence, precisely defined jobs; the more precise the definitions, however, the more easily people can be substituted by machines or by other people. Since information technology is doubling its performance every eighteen months, there is a continuing race between people and technology – one increasingly lost by more qualified people. They are squeezed out of the labour market, leaving behind a rising percentage of "nondescribable" jobs (entrepreneurial, creative, communicative, etc.) which are complementary to technology and hence not subject to the man-machine race. At the same time, the shift makes the organisation less and less mechanistic. Globalisation compounds this development, since well-defined jobs are easily transferable to countries with lower salaries (while largely automatised plants, where a complementary relation between labour and technology prevails, are increasingly "repatriated").

The overall result is that more and more people, and even highly qualified people in well-defined jobs in OECD countries, are laid off – many of them permanently. They are ill-prepared for those jobs which are in increasing demand, because they define themselves instead of being defined from the outside.

Summary and conclusion: the "two-thirds-society"

In summarising the problems at hand, it is possible to say the following:

a) Globalisation – by lowering the tolerance threshold with respect to economic disparities, by facilitating the global mobility of capital, people, and even crime, by multiplying the potential of regional conflicts, and by highlighting the limits of global ecology – creates a tendency to import the North-South conflict into the OECD countries (*Tiermondialisation*) and to make it a negative-sum game for them, since they are importing the problems while exporting the job opportunities.

b) This is aggravating the already existing gap within the OECD between a shrinking majority able to cope with the new challenges of individualisation in jobs, lifestyles and communities, and an increasing minority lacking the skills and competences to orientate themselves in the flood of options and information, to assume nondescribable jobs, or to defend their interests in a pluralist society. Apart from the obvious downward mobility at the margins of the majority, there are virtuous and vicious circles which ensure that the two groups increasingly drift apart and close themselves off, *i.e.* building ghettos.

The majority will tend to live in the countryside – in the new polis – governing themselves in small towns and villages but probably also in the privileged neighbourhoods and historical centres of urban agglomerations. The poor minority will have to withdraw to the declining areas of urban centres with deteriorating public services, where security and health are increasingly affected by crime, street fighting and deprivation; hence, they will eventually be faced with diminishing average life expectancy. The only bridges between the ghettos of the rich and those of the poor will be vice and the servants, the latter being available at low prices.

c) One of the vicious circles relates to the increasing inadequacies of social systems. They are under strain from the sheer weight of these problems, which puts greater pressure on the better-off to finance the poverty ghettos. Since the better-off are convinced it is possible to meet the challenges provided one is prepared to take one's life in hand, and since they regard the poverty ghettos as a desperate world of people without any hope or will to develop themselves, solidarity will fade away. The circle thus formed involves problems and the lack of funds available in quantitative terms; it will also be impossible to invest in the qualitative restructuring of social systems necessary to change them from desperate redistribution machines to problem-solving services.

d) Clearly, this development represents an increasing threat to governability in OECD countries. National states are being undermined by globalisation, continental blocks and regionalisation; meanwhile, the better-off are governing themselves in increasingly autonomous communities, and the poor are frequently under the threat of being governed by organised crime. In order to save a vestige of legitimacy within the framework of diminishing financial means, governments will desperately try to regulate the growing problems of internal and external security and disorder – thus adding regulation conflicts to the increasing load of unsolved problems. This could well set in motion another vicious spiral involving a police state, political radicalisation and anarchy.

e) Behind every one of these problems stands the fact that the patterns of everyday reality, problem-solving and organisation that have been so successful during several centuries of industrialisation have reached and transcended the limits of their validity; the more societies try to do more of the same, the more self-evident this becomes. However, it is also true that the main trends currently observed are themselves already producing new patterns which may point to new solutions: it would seem that the better-off majority in OECD countries is developing a new paradigm that deserves close attention. On the other side of the fence are those who are unable to cope – not only the poor, but also the traditional political, economic and cultural leaders who still consider society and its organisations to be a mechanism over which it is essential to have control. Fear of losing that control blinds them to the fact that what they should (and ultimately will) lose is not control but the illusion of control.

In conclusion, it could be said that Ralf Dahrendorf found an adequate term to describe the problem when he identified a trend towards a ''two-thirds society'', a (shrinking) majority more or less able to cope with and take advantage of future developments, and a (growing) minority vegetating without much of a prospect. This means facing a new kind of class society, with two separate cultures increasingly closing themselves off from each other.

The only positive features of this society may be that its pyramid is upside-down, and that its better-off majority may develop patterns which could show, in the long run, a way out of the difficulties.

3. Reinventing social cohesion

In the process of identifying the trends that constitute threats to social cohesion in OECD Member countries, there emerged glimpses of built-in potential solutions; it is on these that the second part of the paper will concentrate.

A new paradigm

It has been shown that the traditional problem-solving pattern is no longer adequate to deal with the reality it has produced. No longer can the world, society and organisations be considered machines capable of being redesigned and restructured from the top down once they create problems; no longer are well-defined problems handled by well-defined solutions decided by system heads and implemented in a well-defined way by a well-defined organisation, all the while supervised by well-defined controlling mechanisms.

If the traditional concepts are no longer adequate, what is? Instead of mechanisms, the world, society and its organisations have to be considered as living organisms that are developing in a continuous exchange with their environment. This pattern reflects an ongoing learning process that gives deeper meaning to the banal wisdom that life is learning. We will have to live as learning citizens in a learning society.

The typical organisational pattern forming in today's dynamic and increasingly complex world is one of small, self-developing units loosely linked in networks of dynamic interrelations. This pattern can be seen developing in corporations like ABB, in the marketing and logistics networks created by numerous small family enterprises in the Italian textile and leather industry, and in the "new polis" – but it is also forming in the brains of the connected multiminds. It is the way out of the dilemma between complexity and the capacity to decide and to act, the illness of late industrialisation's dinosaurs. It generalises a pattern which saved capitalism from the fate of communism: co-ordination by exchange of information instead of decisions at the top, a method demonstrated for many centuries by the so-called market mechanism.

Introducing this pattern into traditional organisation machines is not an easy task. It presupposes a fundamental change on the part of decision-makers, in both politics and corporations. They need to become catalysts and partners in the dialogue that keeps self-organisation moving – and, as pointed out already, they need to lose the illusion of being in control. For the labour force, consumers, and citizens, the pattern implies a new attitude of responsibility towards one's own life *vis-à-vis* the response one's own acts produce in one's environment.

A paradigm change is a consequence of the old paradigm having reached its limits. That paradigm nonetheless remains valid within its limits, rather like Newtonian physics. Thus, wherever there are big numbers of similar, well-defined tasks and problems to be solved in advance (either because they always occur in the same way or because there will not be enough time to find a solution once they occur), the mechanistic organisation pattern retains its superiority. However, the increasing diversity and volatility of the environment are reducing the number of instances where this still applies, as is the diffusion of the new pattern.

Thus, while it would be irrational to renounce the tremendous advantages of the traditional organisation pattern, the dynamics of the future will develop from other sources. Those OECD countries quickest to learn how to become learning societies and how to set in motion the dynamics of self-development will be the first to find more adequate economic development patterns and a new level of international competitivity.

There are not many concrete measures that can be taken in order to promote self-development, because it results from a cultural process rather than from a well-defined strategy. For this very reason, it is important to point out the key role such dynamics can play in coping with the problems affecting social cohesion in our societies, since cultural processes are both a consequence and a cause of what people say and of the ideas reflected in their acts.

Democracy and subsidiarity

Anywhere citizens participate in shaping their environment, there is an obvious correlation between democracy and subsidiarity – the latter referring to the principle that decisions should be taken at the lowest possible level (in state and private organisations) and that public authorities should assume only those tasks which cannot be performed by private organisations. As the decision-making level lowers and more is left to unofficial bodies, the citizens concerned have more of an opportunity to participate.

As became clear in the discussion of new organisational patterns, individualisation and regionalisation, there is a powerful trend towards geographical and functional decentralisation in public and private institutions – and consequently, a shifting of responsibility and competences to small teams and communities of people in personal contact (even with respect to global virtual communities). This trend is supported by the diffusion of multimedia and interactive networks as the key technology co-shaping society.

The overall diagnosis so far seems to indicate that this trend should be supported wherever possible: strengthening regional and communal autonomy and networking between regions and communities, deregulation, privatisation, public services financed by user charges rather than taxation, shifting entrepreneurial autonomy to small profit centres in corporations, transforming staff services into small enterprises and trade unions or industrial associations into member services, establishing small office, production or sales teams close to their homes and/or their clients, creating virtual organisations where tele-working plays an increasing role – these are all elements of answers to the question of how to develop new structures and processes able to cope with the new dynamics and complexity of our environment.

The ''new handicrafts'' are a good illustration of specific patterns particularly well adapted to future needs and possibilities. *Handicraft* is the traditional way of developing a product (or a service) through individual dialogue with the client; *new* implies fresh opportunities for doing this with the help of modern technology, especially flexible automation, CAD and interactive telecommunication. There is already a progressive diffusion of this pattern in consumer (and particularly investment) goods and services.

The implications are that small teams take care of small groups of clients they often know personally; that there is no longer a separation between sales and product development; that the importance of central or external services delivering those complements that are not part of the core competences of the team is rising; and that each link in the value-adding chain will see dialogue shaping the tailor-made quality of the next steps.

It is easy to imagine that in this pattern (which could be employed in public services as well), the degree of individual participation rises in parallel with the ensuing degree of differentiation – and that this kind of activity is highly suitable for the majority of future OECD countries, while the minority would have to learn to cope with these patterns, whether on the supply or demand side.

Finally, coming back to subsidiarity, it should not be forgotten that the legitimacy problem of public authorities and its consequences are partly due to the belief that the welfare state has the duty and the means to take care of all the problems that are caused by the lack of social cohesion, and that endanger that cohesion further. Redefining what can and should be done by state authorities and what must be left to the responsibility of the individual citizen, of small networks, of NGOs and of the private economy can in itself be helpful.

This is not to say that deregulation and decentralisation are sufficient answers to all the legitimacy problems of political institutions. Those institutions must be preserved, which is to say kept from degenerating into sole defenders of small particular interests seeking short-term equilibria in zero-sum games instead of developing overall long-term concepts or visions around which they could unite motivated citizens. The way to do that is not clear. Perhaps the answer is to organise democratic dialogues about a range of desirable future scenarios for nations, continents, or regions, or even for a community. As long as the traditional political system does not find a way, there should be no surprise that problems are taken care of by other parts of society in a sometimes more, sometimes less helpful way.

Dematerialisation and the global economy

Mass unemployment in Member countries has knocked concerns about world ecology and the ability to sustain economic growth from the top of the agenda. However, unemployment needs to return to the top position, because it is crucial to social cohesion.

First, inasmuch as growth remains a means of creating jobs, it must be sustainable – otherwise, by definition, it will not last. Secondly, because this implies shifting priorities from labour productivity to natural resources productivity, essentially by changing price signals, it could mean more jobs with less growth. Thirdly, since part of the problem is importing global disparities, OECD countries have a vital interest in enlarging the carrying capacity of the global ecology for further economic development in the Third World. Finally, it is in the OECD countries' vital interest to nurture a form of development co-operation that would help stop the waste of resources in developing countries as well, and that aims at an international division of labour permitting Member countries to concentrate on those jobs that, in the framework of a globalised economy, can support their high salaries.

The good news in this context is that a number of trends described so far already point in the direction of a progressive "dematerialisation" of the economy, in several respects; moreover, since long-term interests and trends point the same way, it should be easy for them to gain the support of politicians, trade unions and industrialists. At the same time, however, defenders of the status quo stand united against dematerialisation. Therefore, it may be useful to search actively for realistic visions which demonstrate that there *are* ways out of what now amount to zero-sum games.

Dematerialisation means, first of all, a quantum leap in the productivity of natural resources and of routinised labour through information processing, *i.e.* the development of more "intelligent" materials, procedures, structures and products. While this development is already well under way, helped especially by today's information, materials and bioengineering technologies, the necessary quantum leap is still far off – especially in energy productivity – since price relations are nowhere near producing sufficient incentives to this end.

However, dematerialisation is probably only one necessary condition for sustainability, but not in itself sufficient. There must also be a "culturisation" of the economy:

a) Consumers, workers and citizens must themselves know what they want instead of servicing an economy whose growth is the principal aim. In today's Member countries, for an increasing part of the population, the quality of life is not enhanced simply by being able to buy more of the same, but by developing additional means to shape one's life and environment according to personal aspirations. The real questions are "how" and "what" instead of "how much" – and these are cultural questions, by definition. As a consequence, in goods and services, variety and differentiation are no longer sufficient or profitable. What are increasingly in demand are tailor-made products, at least partly developed in an individual dialogue with the client. This is where the new handicraft comes into the picture. Adding value is becoming less a result of producing more than of responding to specific needs and desires. This new attitude is developing not only with respect to products, but also in relation to working conditions. Work must make sense, be meaningful, contribute to personal development, be fun, produce worthwhile social contacts, etc. In addition, the impact of new technologies and investment projects on the social and natural environments has to be positive for those participating and affected; if such technologies and projects are not developed in ongoing dialogue, they are not acceptable and hence not capable of surviving.

b) The trend towards flexible, loosely knit networks of dynamic relations between small, self-developing units means "cultivating" work in the sense that the art of communicating, of designing social networks, buildings, products and messages, of innovating, of creating, of conceptualising – all these are becoming the core activity all along the value-adding chain. This is especially true at the chain's end, where goods and services increasingly help consumers shape and reinvent their lives.

c) In this perspective, the cultural sector – traditionally speaking, the arts, science, education – becomes a major growth industry. Its products account for an increasing portion of the consumer's budget, and it produces the key production means of the future: languages, media, knowledge, qualifications, lifestyles, design, means of interpreting and evaluating the contemporary environment, understanding different cultures, etc.

d) The less mechanistic and more self-organising our organisations become, the more important their *culture* becomes – the word here refers to a common code which contains the self-description of the organisation in the minds of the people concerned and which acts as the central instrument of co-ordination. In order to remain attuned to a turbulent environment, the culture of an organisation must be the subject of ongoing dialogue in the network.

e) Given the importance of an international division of labour based on the comparative advantages (today one would say ''core competences'') of different regions – and given further that the problem of underdevelopment is, in most cases, due not to the lack of natural resources and capital but to political constellations and advice that impede validation of local natural and cultural resources – intercultural dialogue will become the main instrument of a rational division of labour, permitting both sides, in a process of mutual learning and project development, to discover and concentrate on their particular strengths. This is true in North-South relations and even more so in the East-West configuration, since eastern Europe is in many respects a very highly developed area where co-operation synergies can be tremendous provided they are not stifled by protectionist atavism.

Thus, the final point in this section on dematerialisation must be to underline free trade in goods and services: any protectionist or autarkic reflex impedes that concentration on core competences which is at the root of an efficient – *i.e.* increasingly resources-saving – world economy, and also at the root of today's powerful restructuring movement in private industry.

Rethinking science and education

The emerging new pattern of society and the economy necessitates fundamental changes in science and, far more importantly, educational policy. Astonishingly, although the new paradigm was first discovered by scientists, the sciences have been much slower to adapt their ''culture'' and organisation to that paradigm than the private economy. Without going into detail, the main changes in science policy that are overdue in the light of the trends and necessities described so far are:

- to transcend the compartmentalisation of scientific disciplines;
- to develop questions and answers in dialogue with the users, in politics, the economy, the cultural sector and elsewhere;
- to give more attention to social innovations, as compared to natural sciences and technology, than in the past.

Educational reform is, however, much more important to society than scientific reform. Looking at the changes analysed above, it is probably the single most important field of action, since we are entering the age of the lifelong learning society.

In these circumstances, an education system should do the following:

a) There needs to be a profound shift in the content of learning – away from the knowledge items usually taught, to the general capacity to learn, to a combination of orientation knowledge and special knowledge developed in individual projects, together with personal and social competences, noncognitive dimensions of learning, and learning by doing.

b) This profoundly reshaped learning package should, in principle, be available to everyone, since the only way out of the two-thirds-society is a population able to cope with an increasingly complex and dynamic environment. This means that a special effort will be necessary in the poor neighbourhoods and with respect to those with low educational levels and those from distant cultures. Experiments with interactive media have proved that it is possible to motivate young people practically without any school education to engage in learning projects and a self-developing process that can help make them more emancipated citizens. Unemployed people can also benefit from such efforts. There is a need to develop practical, project-orientated and entertaining learning schemes.

c) Learning – in every respect – is becoming a lifelong process, and it has to be organised as such. Exams and initial professional training are becoming, at best, semi-finished products. The familiar progression of learning-professional life-retirement is becoming a thing of the past. The lifelong learning process will have to continue into old age, and will deal equally with personal development, professional skills, social competence and leisure.

d) Learning will not be limited to teaching situations. Self-teaching with the help of different knowledge sources and media, TV schools and universities, consulting and counselling, learning in project teams, etc. will complement more traditional schemes, and learning will go hand in hand with pleasure, entertainment, living experience and even – literally as well as figuratively – the realisation of one's own visions.

e) This multitude of forms and contexts calls for a multitude of institutions: state and private schools, universities, media, consulting businesses, personal development and project managers, etc. will need to be combined, in a framework of transparency and competition.

It is probably unrealistic to imagine that the leap towards a learning society could be initiated on the basis of one courageous decision by ministers of education acting in unison. However, it will be important that a whole networking fabric of politicians, managers and professionals in education develop this kind of awareness through experimenting, observing, exchanging experiences and sharing innovations, systems and skills in order to make – if not leaps – then at least moves in the right direction.

How to make the labour market work

The core problem with respect to the two-thirds-society is to avoid lasting unemployment and marginalisation of the unemployed and unemployable. The attempt to do so by an overall reduction of labour costs is socially and economically irrational; there are many cases where those costs are merited and sustainable in a competitive world market, and the seemingly contradictory struggles to earn higher salaries and to finance more effective social systems are in fact an important source of innovation and hence of achieving better use of scarce resources.

The real difficulty in tackling the problem is the rigid supply pattern produced by laws and collective bargaining, which stuffs salary structures, working hours and other conditions into a tight corset; the results are rarely those of a healthily functioning market.

The historical reasons for this have increasingly lost their relevance:

- In today's organisations, a rising percentage of employees are capable of knowing what they want and what their opportunities are, and of negotiating on a level equal with that of their employers.
- Both sides have a growing interest in negotiating highly individualised agreements as to where to work (at home, in decentralised offices, at the headquarters, on the road), when to work (hours a week or a day, in what rhythm, with respect to peak hours of sales or machine capacity utilisation, what season, what time in life), and under what kind of contract (pay per hour, lump sum, percentage of profits, as a subcontractor, etc.).
- Those who still need the protection of trade unions are in fact mostly people with inadequate education and skills, and thus constitute the majority of the unemployed. Hence, they are not only not protected, but kept out of the market by the salaries and other rules protecting those workers who "possess" a job and keep the threshold high for others trying to enter the market.
- The same is true for many established rules, including those purportedly protecting female workers.

It is an acknowledged principle, developed in the discussion about ecology, that markets only operate in the general interest if, among other things, the actors are obliged to assume the consequences of their acts. Currently, trade unions heavily influence the labour supply structure, while the results are borne by companies and the labour force.

Thus, a profound review of the function of trade unions would seem appropriate. The result could be that they act as service organisations helping their members to develop the skills and know-how they need as equal partners in the negotiation with employers, and watching that new forms of abuse of their "clients" by employers, which could well develop in a framework of "new flexibility", are avoided – by law, if necessary. They could equally play an important role in the development of new networks enabling the labour force to acquire adequate professional skills during lifelong learning as well as during the adjustment process, one in which virtually everyone will increasingly be involved.

The building of a highly differentiated, flexible network of lifelong development is, of course, a central pillar in such a strategy leading towards an ideally functioning labour market.

Even if doubts remain over its political feasibility, this strategy may be approached step by step once the vision is established. One extremely important combined step would be to restrict collective bargaining to jobs not yet fully individualised; to differentiate agreements according to labour productivity in individual industries or, preferably, enterprises; and to limit those agreements to questions regarding the share of the productivity gains that should (after making allowances for changes in the terms of trade) be attributed to the employees, leaving to individual negotiations the form such gains should take (pay, reduced working hours, capital shares, etc.).

Eliminating rigidities on the supply side will necessitate not only a change in the role of trade unions, but also a review of the legal framework. Restrictions of all kinds, especially on working hours, holidays, etc. will need to be re-examined; only those genuinely necessary for health and security reasons should be retained.

Certainly, there are rigidities on the demand side as well. However, with the exception of public administrations and legally protected professions – areas which should be radically reviewed for their flexibility potential – these reside mainly in a certain laziness or lack of imagination on the part of employers. Here, the main action would be an overall strategy of radical deregulation and elimination of all impediments to competition, a necessary complement of flexible labour markets. Competition will also increasingly eliminate those employers still living in a world without contemporary administration software and claiming that flexible working conditions are simply too complicated to manage.

A strategy of deregulation and arranging greater flexibility alone would, in fact, eliminate some of the problems of social cohesion identified above. It must be stressed that with regard to social cohesion, the effects of improving market efficiency are not negative but positive, since such improvement:

1. increases overall productivity and purchasing power;
2. opens a broader range of opportunities, even for less-qualified people;
3. eliminates protectionist thresholds to market entry.

This is particularly true if the strategy is combined with educational reform that allows increasing numbers of people to enter the labour market as autonomous suppliers.

There is no claim that the actions discussed so far would eliminate all kinds of social disruption. If, in addition, there is no reason to believe there will be a huge, OECD-wide movement towards the new frontiers of a coming cultural age, it must be concluded that the two-thirds-society will be around for decades to come. Adequate forms of social solidarity will therefore be needed. The welfare state is here to stay, but profound reshaping is called for if it is to tackle the problems at hand.

Perspectives for the marginalised

How should social security and service systems be organised in order:

1. to permit a decent life for those ill-equipped to cope with the problems of our complex civilisation;
2. to do the utmost to integrate or reintegrate the highest possible number of people in difficulty;
3. not to interfere with the functioning of the labour market;

4. to support the aim of maximum flexibility in everyone's options to shape his or her life?

The answer has to be sought in a combination of features:

1. It is necessary to eliminate the digitalisation of our social systems, *i.e.* the fact that one is either active or not (unemployed, retired, handicapped, etc.) – at least officially.
2. Everyone should be entitled to minimal support that guarantees basic subsistence while not eliminating the motivation to work.
3. Integration is not just a question of financial support but also one of social and educational services.
4. Transfer payments for social reasons should be separated from insurance and pension schemes for the better-off.

The consequences are self-evident:

1. There must be a basic network of financial social security, following Milton Friedman's concept of negative income tax. At zero income, people would get a minimum level of support which would be reduced progressively in accordance with earnings, reaching zero at a low but decent income level, and be financed by the progressive positive taxes to be payed from there on. This scheme should, in principle, replace all other social security payments. It would eliminate the digitalisation mentioned above, maintain the impetus to earn more, and support the flexibility of working arrangements throughout life. It would be especially worthwhile for mothers or fathers assuming professional and parental responsibilities at the same time. Of course, replacing existing systems with this scheme will be extremely difficult. However, it could be done gradually; establishing a mix between unemployment benefits and part-time salaries could be a first step.
2. The demand for social security payments to maintain the standard of living a person has reached in the course of his or her biography should be satisfied by additional insurance schemes financed by those taking advantage of them, either individually or collectively; this could be organised on a private and competitive basis.
3. The financial schemes must be combined with social services helping the needy and the unemployed to cope with their daily lives, to reshape their qualifications and, if possible, to look for a job, even if this amounts to occasional part-time work. It could be useful to create a financial incentive to participate in reorientation schemes, like the *Beschäftigungsgesellschaften* in Germany. These reintegration services should be developed with the best know-how and imagination available in order to maintain high levels of motivation.
4. Since there will be tremendous demand for all kinds of social services, governments might think of introducing a general public service duty during periods of unemployment.

Technology helps

Technology is a core factor in all the social innovations mentioned in this paper:

- Interactive telecommunication networks and multimedia are a condition for new, decentralised and flexible organisation patterns in the economy, in politics, in culture and in housing.
- The combination of interactive telecommunication, CAD and flexible automation is a central pillar in the new tailor-made shaping of products, services and working conditions.
- Information, bioengineering, materials and process optimisation technologies are essential to the more "intelligent" and hence dematerialising materials, structures, processes and products of the economy.
- Accumulating the results of these applications and delegating the routine to automation enables OECD countries to concentrate on their core competences and to preserve, if not increase, their standard of living in global competition.

What, then, is the role of government in technology? In line with the principle of subsidiarity, on a European if not global level, it should be:

- to develop a vision of future technological infrastructures;
- accordingly, to serve as catalyst in developing the necessary global standards (for example, HDTV);
- to realise a basic communication highway, which is to say a global integrated services digital network (ISDN), without interfering in local and company extensions;
- to develop, in the dialogue with suppliers and users, the necessary standards and rules for horizontal value-added services, possibly even on a user-pays basis;
- to promote, in the framework of mixed private-public organisations and especially on a local level, experiments and pilot projects leading to technology applications which may prove to be socially useful without being profitable, at least in the short run;
- to ensure that the transition from the information age to the cultural age and the realm of public services undergoing that transition will indeed be governed by the principles of subsidiarity, the free market and personal autonomy, and that apart from the case of public services, competition will not be overruled by private or public monopolies.

Summary and conclusion: redefining government

A recurring theme throughout this paper is that government does not play the central role either in creating problems or in solving them; nevertheless, it is an important actor whose task in dealing with them may be summarised as follows.

One difficulty is the increasing discrepancy between the alleged and actual problem-solving capacity of governments. The answer is a reconceptualisation of governmental tasks, from the perspective of subsidiarity: what are the essential duties of government and what may constitute additional core competences justifying additional activities?

This kind of reconceptualisation must include subsidiarity in the geographical sense as well. While many problems call for a shift of co-operation or even state sovereignty to continental and global levels, an increasing number of them could be dealt with more efficiently and democratically on a regional or local level.

Reconceptualisation of government has an immediate bearing on social cohesion since, as has been shown, the main factor behind social disruption is the inability (of individuals as well as private and public organisations) to cope with accelerating change and diversity. Deregulation and flexibilisation are key notions here. However, organisation of government itself along the emerging patterns, and of new modes of participatory decision-making, are also part of the redefining process.

More concretely, there are a range of government activities that would help to overcome the otherwise inevitable development of a two-thirds-society, the most important of which are profound educational reform and a rethinking of the welfare state.

The whole set of government actions proposed throughout this paper must be viewed against a reality in which the more government legitimacy is questioned, the more the united status-quo defenders lock themselves in their fortress – still solidly built from the bricks of small particular interests – and defy the rising flood of diversity. Thus, the main task may be to unite those forces (both inside and outside government) that consider turbulence and emerging new patterns of behaviour and organisation as an opportunity rather than as a threat, and form a broad-based democratic dialogue with the aim of developing new visions and concepts of "Western" society following the fall of the Soviet Empire – an event which left us with the illusion that we would not be forced to rethink *our* society.

OECD Forum for the Future
"OECD Societies in Transition: The Future of Work and Leisure"

PARTICIPANTS

Koos ANDRIESSEN
Minister for Economic Affairs
Netherlands

Richard H. BLANDY
Director
Institute of Applied Economic and Social Research
University of Melbourne
Australia

Friedrich BUTTLER
Director, Institute of Employment Research
Federal Employment Services
Germany

Fernando CLAVIJO
Co-ordinator for Economic Affairs
President's Office
Mexico

Guillermo DE LA DEHESA ROMERO
Chief Executive Officer
Banco Pastor
President, Confederation of the Spanish Chambers of Commerce and Industry
Spain

Frank DOYLE
Executive Vice President
General Electric Company
United States

Pierre FONTAINE
Sous-ministre adjoint
Ministère de la Main-d'œuvre, de la Sécurité du revenu
et de la Formation professionnelle, Québec
Canada

Emilio FONTELA
Professor of Economics
Universities of Madrid and Geneva
Spain/Switzerland

Robert GOEBBELS
Ministre de l'Économie, des Travaux Publics et des Transports
Luxembourg

Gudmund HERNES
Minister of Church, Education and Research
Norway

Sumiko IWAO
Professor for Social Psychology
Keio University
Japan

Yuriko KAWAGUCHI
Managing Director
Suntori Limited
Japan

Hans LENK
Professor of Philosophy
University of Karlsruhe
Germany

Jacques LESOURNE
Directeur
Le Monde
France

Christian LUTZ
Managing Director
Gottlieb Duttweiler Institute for Social and Economic Studies
Switzerland

Graham L. REID
Deputy Secretary
Department of Employment
United Kingdom

Alan REYNOLDS
Director of Economic Research
Hudson Institute
United States

Jonathan M. SILVER
Assistant Deputy Secretary
Department of Commerce
United States

Kari TAPIOLA
International Secretary
Central Organisation of Finnish Trade Unions (SAK)
Finland

William WALLACE
St. Antony's College
University of Oxford
United Kingdom

Eric WANNER
President
Russell Sage Foundation
United States

Bengt WESTERBERG
Deputy Prime Minister
Minister of Social Affairs
Sweden

OECD SECRETARIAT

Jean-Claude PAYE
Secretary-General

Makoto TANIGUCHI
Deputy Secretary-General

Wolfgang MICHALSKI
Head of the Advisory Unit to the Secretary-General

MAIN SALES OUTLETS OF OECD PUBLICATIONS
PRINCIPAUX POINTS DE VENTE DES PUBLICATIONS DE L'OCDE

ARGENTINA – ARGENTINE
Carlos Hirsch S.R.L.
Galería Güemes, Florida 165, 4° Piso
1333 Buenos Aires   Tel. (1) 331.1787 y 331.2391
Telefax: (1) 331.1787

AUSTRALIA – AUSTRALIE
D.A. Information Services
648 Whitehorse Road, P.O.B 163
Mitcham, Victoria 3132   Tel. (03) 873.4411
Telefax: (03) 873.5679

AUSTRIA – AUTRICHE
Gerold & Co.
Graben 31
Wien I   Tel. (0222) 533.50.14

BELGIUM – BELGIQUE
Jean De Lannoy
Avenue du Roi 202
B-1060 Bruxelles   Tel. (02) 538.51.69/538.08.41
Telefax: (02) 538.08.41

CANADA
Renouf Publishing Company Ltd.
1294 Algoma Road
Ottawa, ON K1B 3W8   Tel. (613) 741.4333
Telefax: (613) 741.5439
Stores:
61 Sparks Street
Ottawa, ON K1P 5R1   Tel. (613) 238.8985
211 Yonge Street
Toronto, ON M5B 1M4   Tel. (416) 363.3171
Telefax: (416)363.59.63
Les Éditions La Liberté Inc.
3020 Chemin Sainte-Foy
Sainte-Foy, PQ G1X 3V6   Tel. (418) 658.3763
Telefax: (418) 658.3763

Federal Publications Inc.
165 University Avenue, Suite 701
Toronto, ON M5H 3B8   Tel. (416) 860.1611
Telefax: (416) 860.1608
Les Publications Fédérales
1185 Université
Montréal, QC H3B 3A7   Tel. (514) 954.1633
Telefax : (514) 954.1635

CHINA – CHINE
China National Publications Import
Export Corporation (CNPIEC)
16 Gongti E. Road, Chaoyang District
P.O. Box 88 or 50
Beijing 100704 PR   Tel. (01) 506.6688
Telefax: (01) 506.3101

DENMARK – DANEMARK
Munksgaard Book and Subscription Service
35, Nørre Søgade, P.O. Box 2148
DK-1016 København K   Tel. (33) 12.85.70
Telefax: (33) 12.93.87

FINLAND – FINLANDE
Akateeminen Kirjakauppa
Keskuskatu 1, P.O. Box 128
00100 Helsinki
Subscription Services/Agence d'abonnements :
P.O. Box 23
00371 Helsinki   Tel. (358 0) 12141
Telefax: (358 0) 121.4450

FRANCE
OECD/OCDE
Mail Orders/Commandes par correspondance:
2, rue André-Pascal
75775 Paris Cedex 16   Tel. (33-1) 45.24.82.00
Telefax: (33-1) 49.10.42.76
Telex: 640048 OCDE

OECD Bookshop/Librairie de l'OCDE :
33, rue Octave-Feuillet
75016 Paris   Tel. (33-1) 45.24.81.67
(33-1) 45.24.81.81
Documentation Française
29, quai Voltaire
75007 Paris   Tel. 40.15.70.00
Gibert Jeune (Droit-Économie)
6, place Saint-Michel
75006 Paris   Tel. 43.25.91.19
Librairie du Commerce International
10, avenue d'Iéna
75016 Paris   Tel. 40.73.34.60
Librairie Dunod
Université Paris-Dauphine
Place du Maréchal de Lattre de Tassigny
75016 Paris   Tel. (1) 44.05.40.13
Librairie Lavoisier
11, rue Lavoisier
75008 Paris   Tel. 42.65.39.95
Librairie L.G.D.J. - Montchrestien
20, rue Soufflot
75005 Paris   Tel. 46.33.89.85
Librairie des Sciences Politiques
30, rue Saint-Guillaume
75007 Paris   Tel. 45.48.36.02
P.U.F.
49, boulevard Saint-Michel
75005 Paris   Tel. 43.25.83.40
Librairie de l'Université
12a, rue Nazareth
13100 Aix-en-Provence   Tel. (16) 42.26.18.08
Documentation Française
165, rue Garibaldi
69003 Lyon   Tel. (16) 78.63.32.23
Librairie Decitre
29, place Bellecour
69002 Lyon   Tel. (16) 72.40.54.54

GERMANY – ALLEMAGNE
OECD Publications and Information Centre
August-Bebel-Allee 6
D-53175 Bonn   Tel. (0228) 959.120
Telefax: (0228) 959.12.17

GREECE – GRÈCE
Librairie Kauffmann
Mavrokordatou 9
106 78 Athens   Tel. (01) 32.55.321
Telefax: (01) 36.33.967

HONG-KONG
Swindon Book Co. Ltd.
13–15 Lock Road
Kowloon, Hong Kong   Tel. 366.80.31
Telefax: 739.49.75

HUNGARY – HONGRIE
Euro Info Service
Margitsziget, Európa Ház
1138 Budapest   Tel. (1) 111.62.16
Telefax : (1) 111.60.61

ICELAND – ISLANDE
Mál Mog Menning
Laugavegi 18, Pósthólf 392
121 Reykjavik   Tel. 162.35.23

INDIA – INDE
Oxford Book and Stationery Co.
Scindia House
New Delhi 110001   Tel.(11) 331.5896/5308
Telefax: (11) 332.5993
17 Park Street
Calcutta 700016   Tel. 240832

INDONESIA – INDONÉSIE
Pdii-Lipi
P.O. Box 269/JKSMG/88
Jakarta 12790   Tel. 583467
Telex: 62 875

ISRAEL
Praedicta
5 Shatner Street
P.O. Box 34030
Jerusalem 91430   Tel. (2) 52.84.90/1/2
Telefax: (2) 52.84.93
R.O.Y.
P.O. Box 13056
Tel Aviv 61130   Tél. (3) 49.61.08
Telefax (3) 544.60.39

ITALY – ITALIE
Libreria Commissionaria Sansoni
Via Duca di Calabria 1/1
50125 Firenze   Tel. (055) 64.54.15
Telefax: (055) 64.12.57
Via Bartolini 29
20155 Milano   Tel. (02) 36.50.83
Editrice e Libreria Herder
Piazza Montecitorio 120
00186 Roma   Tel. 679.46.28
Telefax: 678.47.51
Libreria Hoepli
Via Hoepli 5
20121 Milano   Tel. (02) 86.54.46
Telefax: (02) 805.28.86
Libreria Scientifica
Dott. Lucio de Biasio 'Aeiou'
Via Coronelli, 6
20146 Milano   Tel. (02) 48.95.45.52
Telefax: (02) 48.95.45.48

JAPAN – JAPON
OECD Publications and Information Centre
Landic Akasaka Building
2-3-4 Akasaka, Minato-ku
Tokyo 107   Tel. (81.3) 3586.2016
Telefax: (81.3) 3584.7929

KOREA – CORÉE
Kyobo Book Centre Co. Ltd.
P.O. Box 1658, Kwang Hwa Moon
Seoul   Tel. 730.78.91
Telefax: 735.00.30

MALAYSIA – MALAISIE
Co-operative Bookshop Ltd.
University of Malaya
P.O. Box 1127, Jalan Pantai Baru
59700 Kuala Lumpur
Malaysia   Tel. 756.5000/756.5425
Telefax: 757.3661

MEXICO – MEXIQUE
Revistas y Periodicos Internacionales S.A. de C.V.
Florencia 57 - 1004
Mexico, D.F. 06600   Tel. 207.81.00
Telefax : 208.39.79

NETHERLANDS – PAYS-BAS
SDU Uitgeverij Plantijnstraat
Externe Fondsen
Postbus 20014
2500 EA's-Gravenhage   Tel. (070) 37.89.880
Voor bestellingen: Telefax: (070) 34.75.778

NEW ZEALAND
NOUVELLE-ZÉLANDE
Legislation Services
P.O. Box 12418
Thorndon, Wellington   Tel. (04) 496.5652
Telefax: (04) 496.5698

NORWAY – NORVÈGE
Narvesen Info Center – NIC
Bertrand Narvesens vei 2
P.O. Box 6125 Etterstad
0602 Oslo 6   Tel. (022) 57.33.00
                                     Telefax: (022) 68.19.01

PAKISTAN
Mirza Book Agency
65 Shahrah Quaid-E-Azam
Lahore 54000   Tel. (42) 353.601
                                     Telefax: (42) 231.730

PHILIPPINE – PHILIPPINES
International Book Center
5th Floor, Filipinas Life Bldg.
Ayala Avenue
Metro Manila   Tel. 81.96.76
                                     Telex 23312 RHP PH

PORTUGAL
Livraria Portugal
Rua do Carmo 70-74
Apart. 2681
1200 Lisboa   Tel.: (01) 347.49.82/5
                                     Telefax: (01) 347.02.64

SINGAPORE – SINGAPOUR
Gower Asia Pacific Pte Ltd.
Golden Wheel Building
41, Kallang Pudding Road, No. 04-03
Singapore 1334   Tel. 741.5166
                                     Telefax: 742.9356

SPAIN – ESPAGNE
Mundi-Prensa Libros S.A.
Castelló 37, Apartado 1223
Madrid 28001   Tel. (91) 431.33.99
                                     Telefax: (91) 575.39.98

Libreria Internacional AEDOS
Consejo de Ciento 391
08009 – Barcelona   Tel. (93) 488.30.09
                                     Telefax: (93) 487.76.59

Llibreria de la Generalitat
Palau Moja
Rambla dels Estudis, 118
08002 – Barcelona
                 (Subscripcions) Tel. (93) 318.80.12
                 (Publicacions) Tel. (93) 302.67.23
                                     Telefax: (93) 412.18.54

SRI LANKA
Centre for Policy Research
c/o Colombo Agencies Ltd.
No. 300-304, Galle Road
Colombo 3   Tel. (1) 574240, 573551-2
                                     Telefax: (1) 575394, 510711

SWEDEN – SUÈDE
Fritzes Information Center
Box 16356
Regeringsgatan 12
106 47 Stockholm   Tel. (08) 690.90.90
                                     Telefax: (08) 20.50.21
Subscription Agency/Agence d'abonnements :
Wennergren-Williams Info AB
P.O. Box 1305
171 25 Solna   Tel. (08) 705.97.50
                                     Téléfax : (08) 27.00.71

SWITZERLAND – SUISSE
Maditec S.A. (Books and Periodicals - Livres
et périodiques)
Chemin des Palettes 4
Case postale 266
1020 Renens   Tel. (021) 635.08.65
                                     Telefax: (021) 635.07.80

Librairie Payot S.A.
4, place Pépinet
CP 3212
1002 Lausanne   Tel. (021) 341.33.48
                                     Telefax: (021) 341.33.45

Librairie Unilivres
6, rue de Candolle
1205 Genève   Tel. (022) 320.26.23
                                     Telefax: (022) 329.73.18

Subscription Agency/Agence d'abonnements :
Dynapresse Marketing S.A.
38 avenue Vibert
1227 Carouge   Tel.: (022) 308.07.89
                                     Telefax : (022) 308.07.99

See also – Voir aussi :
OECD Publications and Information Centre
August-Bebel-Allee 6
D-53175 Bonn (Germany)   Tel. (0228) 959.120
                                     Telefax: (0228) 959.12.17

TAIWAN – FORMOSE
Good Faith Worldwide Int'l. Co. Ltd.
9th Floor, No. 118, Sec. 2
Chung Hsiao E. Road
Taipei   Tel. (02) 391.7396/391.7397
                                     Telefax: (02) 394.9176

THAILAND – THAÏLANDE
Suksit Siam Co. Ltd.
113, 115 Fuang Nakhon Rd.
Opp. Wat Rajbopith
Bangkok 10200   Tel. (662) 225.9531/2
                                     Telefax: (662) 222.5188

TURKEY – TURQUIE
Kültür Yayinlari Is-Türk Ltd. Sti.
Atatürk Bulvari No. 191/Kat 13
Kavaklidere/Ankara   Tel. 428.11.40 Ext. 2458
Dolmabahce Cad. No. 29
Besiktas/Istanbul   Tel. 260.71.88
                                     Telex: 43482B

UNITED KINGDOM – ROYAUME-UNI
HMSO
Gen. enquiries   Tel. (071) 873 0011
Postal orders only:
P.O. Box 276, London SW8 5DT
Personal Callers HMSO Bookshop
49 High Holborn, London WC1V 6HB
                                     Telefax: (071) 873 8200
Branches at: Belfast, Birmingham, Bristol, Edin-
burgh, Manchester

UNITED STATES – ÉTATS-UNIS
OECD Publications and Information Centre
2001 L Street N.W., Suite 700
Washington, D.C. 20036-4910 Tel. (202) 785.6323
                                     Telefax: (202) 785.0350

VENEZUELA
Libreria del Este
Avda F. Miranda 52, Aptdo. 60337
Edificio Galipán
Caracas 106   Tel. 951.1705/951.2307/951.1297
                                     Telegram: Libreste Caracas

Subscription to OECD periodicals may also be
placed through main subscription agencies.

Les abonnements aux publications périodiques de
l'OCDE peuvent être souscrits auprès des
principales agences d'abonnement.

Orders and inquiries from countries where Distribu-
tors have not yet been appointed should be sent to:
OECD Publications Service, 2 rue André-Pascal,
75775 Paris Cedex 16, France.

Les commandes provenant de pays où l'OCDE n'a
pas encore désigné de distributeur devraient être
adressées à : OCDE, Service des Publications,
2, rue André-Pascal, 75775 Paris Cedex 16, France.

9-1994

OECD PUBLICATIONS, 2 rue André-Pascal, 75775 PARIS CEDEX 16
PRINTED IN FRANCE
(03 94 05 1) ISBN 92-64-14256-8 - No. 47163 1994